KT-407-941

Matron On Call

Matron On Call

More true stories of a 1960s nurse

JOAN WOODCOCK

headline

First published in 2012
by HEADLINE PUBLISHING GROUP

1

Cataloguing in Publication Data is available from the British Library

ISBN 978 0 7553 6152 6

Typeset in Dante by Avon DataSet Ltd,
Bidford-on-Avon, Warwickshire

Printed and bound by CPI Group (UK) Ltd, Croydon, CR0 4YY

Headline's policy is to use papers that are natural, renewable and
recyclable products and made from wood grown in sustainable forests.
The logging and manufacturing processes are expected to conform
to the environmental regulations of the country of origin.

HEADLINE PUBLISHING GROUP
An Hachette UK Company
338 Euston Road
London NW1 3BH

www.headline.co.uk
www.hachette.co.uk

This book is dedicated to my uncomplaining husband Bill,
without whose enormous help and support this book
would not have been completed

Acknowledgements

Special thanks to my editor Carly for successfully rendering my humble efforts into a state fit for publication; to Emily, Jo and the team at Headline for their constant support; and to my agent Luigi for his original belief in my story, which made it all possible.

Thanks also to my colleagues Jeanne and Jenny for reminding me of the many colourful characters and incidents which were such a feature of life in Casualty when we all worked together at Wythenshawe Hospital. I would like to express my appreciation to all the dedicated doctors, nurses, receptionists, porters and police officers it was my privilege to work with at that time.

And finally to the thousands of patients who sat waiting quietly for countless hours without a word of complaint, thank you for your patience and understanding.

Introduction

My very first contact with an emergency casualty patient was as a sixteen-year-old cadet nurse straight from school, when an elderly lady had been attacked and hit in the face with an axe. The horrific injury turned my stomach but I was surprised that I could still continue to carry out my duties. Commencing formal training at the age of eighteen to become a State Registered Nurse included a three-month period in Blackburn Royal Infirmary's Casualty department, working alongside highly qualified doctors and nurses. Such an acute environment was a scary experience, but it was comforting to know that each student was always kept under close supervision. As a student nurse I was regularly volunteered to clean up the occasional infested/incontinent vagrant before they were examined by a doctor; and mopping up blood and vomit from the floor was all in a day's work.

After qualifying in 1971, marrying in 1972 and starting a family in 1974, I worked at several different hospitals in

Lancashire including the Casualty department at Blackpool Victoria Hospital. Relocation to Cheshire in 1983 saw me commence in the busy Casualty department at Wythenshawe Hospital in South Manchester where I learnt a great deal, encountered lots of different characters and experienced many challenging situations over the next six years.

A busy Accident and Emergency department is a contrasting mixture of routine treatments for countless mundane minor injuries interspersed with urgent life-saving team action. In my experience, the way this is portrayed to the public on television as a hectic scrum, in which everyone is shouting at the tops of their voices and running around avoiding the spurting blood, is totally misleading and the reality is a much less dramatic but quietly assured and measured response. Meanwhile, the unfortunate victims of serious accidents are inevitably in deep shock and disorientated, and often unconscious. I recently heard their experience described (obviously light-heartedly, but still quite aptly) in this way: 'One minute you are riding along on your bike, quietly minding your own business, then the next minute you wake up stark naked, strapped to a stretcher, with a complete stranger poking their finger up your bottom.'

This book is a compilation of true stories and recollections brought together from my six years at Wythenshawe Hospital in the 80s into one busy shift on New Year's Eve – a night that is generally regarded by all the emergency services as one of the busiest and most stressful of the year. The names of patients and some staff have been changed to protect confidentiality, although many other names of individuals have been retained as a tribute to their dedication and professionalism.

Chapter 1

5.15pm

I must have been barmy! Heaven knows what was going through my mind when I volunteered to work on New Year's Eve. Instead of looking forward to a night curled up on the settee watching one of the endlessly repeated film classics and slurping a nice bottle of red, I was showered and changed into my freshly laundered staff nurse's uniform preparing to go out into the arctic night air.

Because of the unique and infinitely variable workload of a busy Casualty department, I worked a slightly unusual 'twilight' shift that began at 6.00pm and ended at 2.30am. These hours covered what were usually the busiest periods in the department, in addition to covering the handover between the day and night shifts. Working the early part of my shift with the day staff and the rest of the shift with the night staff was enjoyable in many ways, although each shift operated a little differently, which I initially found slightly confusing. The day shift normally had more staff on duty, including three doctors, so the nurses were allocated to work in specific areas. In other words, we'd be assigned to minor injuries, stretchers or the observation ward. More importantly, though, you were expected to stay and work in that particular area for the duration of your shift. In comparison, on night shift there was only ever one casualty doctor on duty and, more often than not, fewer nurses than worked during the day, so it was a matter of helping out where and when you were most needed.

When I first started work at the hospital, some of the day staff gave me odd looks if I absentmindedly strayed from my allocated position, but I honestly didn't do it on purpose. I just couldn't get used to the idea that I should remain in a quiet area when another part of the department was busy with nurses flying around like whirlwinds. I simply wasn't used to standing around and watching while others did the work; I liked to be busy.

If I was lucky, I finished on time at 2.30am, although it was often much later than that and it was far from unusual for me to still be in the thick of it until well after 3am. But I genuinely enjoyed the work and, to be honest, I hadn't yet done the New Year's Eve shift since first starting at Wythenshawe Hospital after moving to South Manchester some four years earlier, so it was probably about time I did!

★

I loved my house in Sale, which we had bought when my husband Bill was promoted to a new job in the area. Growing up in Blackburn in the 1950s with my mum, dad and sister in a small, run-down, terraced property with only an outside toilet, I never imagined that I would ever find myself living in a beautiful, four-bedroom, detached house in a leafy Cheshire suburb. Becoming a nurse had been my only dream and ambition since being hospitalised at the age of four, and I had now been a qualified nurse for over fifteen years. The shy, naïve sixteen-year-old schoolgirl who started training as a cadet all those years ago had transformed somewhere along the way into a virtually unshockable professional who thrived on the pressures of the busy Casualty department of a major teaching hospital.

Bill had just bought me an expensive new winter coat for Christmas, which I wouldn't normally have dreamt of wearing to go to work, but I decided that tonight definitely merited an exception to the rule – it was brass monkeys outside! The ever-cheerful weatherman on Granada Reports had predicted continuing sub-zero temperatures and a glance through the lounge window confirmed an earlier light snowfall was already freezing hard. Realising that completing my journey safely was likely to take much longer in the icy conditions, I decided to set off early; after all, I didn't want to turn up at work as yet another accident statistic. Wrapping myself up tightly against the bitter cold, I shouted a cheery goodbye to my son Mark, who was upstairs in his bedroom doing whatever it is teenagers do to avoid their parents. The path resembled a skating rink and every step was potentially lethal so, with an expectant smirk on his face, Bill watched me inch my way gingerly along to the car. (It never did take much to make me slip and fall, even when I was a child. On literally countless occasions, I have ended up firmly on my backside whenever there is any ice and snow about.)

Needless to say, the car was frozen solid under a crispy white coating and I couldn't even get the key in the lock. The rubber seal around the door seemed to be welded shut but a kettle of hot water eventually defrosted them both. If anything, it felt even colder inside my little yellow Mini than it did outside. And yet, surprisingly, the engine turned over and started almost immediately, although it was coughing and spluttering like an old chronic bronchitic in desperate need of medication. My hands were now almost numb with cold but I eventually cleared a hole in the ice on the windscreen large enough to peer out and see where I was going. My dear husband was now standing at the window wafting a large glass of something rather tasty in my general direction, so as I carefully reversed off the drive I made a mental note to exact retribution in the early hours by planting my icy cold feet on his back when I got back home to my bed.

Turning out on to the main road I was thankful that it had been heavily gritted and there was little traffic, but I had to stop at the roadside about a hundred yards further on when the windscreen iced up again. The best part of a can of de-icer later, I continued along the unusually quiet streets as far as the traffic lights at Brooklands Station, where three or four passengers fleetingly emerged before rapidly scattering into the night, hunched against the cold, leaving only faint traces of frosted breath in their wake.

Most sensible people had obviously decided to stay at home in the warm or were getting ready to hit the town to see in the new year because I completed my journey in what must have been a record time and, for once, instead of fighting heavy traffic, there was an opportunity to appreciate the multitude of brightly coloured festive lights and highly decorated Christmas trees glimpsed through the open curtains of the houses along the way.

Christmas is my favourite time of year and always brings back so many happy memories of my childhood, despite the fact that in those post-war years we had little money and received few presents. I can vividly remember helping Mum to make paper chains by gluing together strips of coloured paper while Dad retrieved our small artificial tree from the loft, where it had been carefully stored since the previous year and which my sister and I then helped to decorate.

As a child it never crossed my mind that my sister or I were ever deprived in any way, though money must always have been tight for our parents. My one abiding memory of Christmas was receiving a gleaming scooter as a present when I was about five or six years old. It was only many years later that Mum told me how Dad had bought a second-hand scooter for me because they couldn't afford a new one and had then spent countless hours in his shed cleaning it, getting rid of the rust and painting it bright red.

New Year's Eve was a bit special, too, because Mum always cooked a huge meat and potato pie each year in a dish that would barely fit into the oven, and which then fed many of our relatives and half our neighbours on the street that night.

When I eventually pulled into the small car park situated directly opposite Casualty entrance, for a split second I seriously considered turning around and going back home; I was chilled to the bone and wanted nothing more than to relax with my family in front of a blazing fire. However, I could never let my colleagues down. Since I had arrived with plenty of time to spare, though, I would just have to get the kettle on and make a hot drink to warm myself up before starting my shift and getting on with it.

The hospital was situated in an area that had become run down and subject to a great deal of petty crime so, before switching off the engine and unlocking the doors, I carefully checked the car park, as per police advice, just in case there was a deranged individual with evil intentions lurking in the shadows. It wasn't a very well-lit area and sometimes groups of youths congregated there. Thankfully all seemed quiet tonight; it was much too cold to be wrestling on the ground with some little toe-rag teenager trying to nick my handbag. With one final glance around I collected up my belongings, ensuring that nothing was left on display that would entice a would-be thief, switched off the engine and locked the car.

How times had changed. When I first worked shifts as an eighteen-year-old student in Blackburn you could get on a late-night bus without a second thought for your safety because a nurse was held in high regard by the general public and the uniform was well respected. In the rare event of anyone causing problems, they would more than likely be challenged immediately by another passenger or a passer-by. Nowadays, the rapidly growing trend in some inner-city areas was for addicts to attack and rob on-call doctors, district nurses and midwives in an attempt to steal medication from their bags. Sadly such disrespect had also extended to most of the emergency services, and ambulance personnel coming out of a house after attending a 999 call regularly had to eject youths looking for drugs in the back of their emergency vehicle. Meanwhile, police officers frequently have to bite their lips when being verbally abused openly by youngsters who no longer fear a good old-fashioned clip round the ear; a friend in the Fire Service told me how he now has to stand guard over his vehicle at the scene of a fire to prevent youths putting a brick through the windscreen.

★

It was an unwritten rule in every hospital where I have worked that anyone on duty either on Christmas Eve or New Year's Eve brings in party food. Ever the optimists, some staff even believe they might actually get a quiet moment to sit down and enjoy eating it at some stage during the evening. My contribution to the feast, consisting of a variety of sandwiches and a huge trifle, was locked safely away in the boot of my car until required. It was probably colder outside than it was in the staff room fridge and, quite honestly, any food left hanging around in the department for long would more than likely have gone walkabout anyway – anything edible has always been considered fair game to any passing hungry doctor or member of staff from another department. I remember one nurse who, having gone to the staff room for her lunch break, found the sandwiches she had left in the fridge eaten and the empty packets strewn around the floor.

Glancing across the road towards Casualty entrance, I could see that business was already quite brisk. Both the adult and the children's waiting rooms were buzzing with activity and there was the usual queue of potential patients at reception waiting to book themselves in. Several adults were already pacing up and down outside puffing frantic- ally on their cigarettes, which was never a good sign as it usually signalled a level of boredom and frustration because they had been kept waiting. This could turn quickly into downright hostility and aggression, especially when alcohol reared its ugly head, as it so often did. Over the years I had become quite adept at reading a patient's body language; it usually proved to be a pretty reliable indication of their mood and regularly helped me to avoid potentially confrontational situations. The trick was always to keep calm and to never raise your voice, to show empathy for their situation and promise to try and help where possible. It was simple enough advice and, amazingly, worked most of the time.

As I crossed the road from the car park, I couldn't quite take in what I was seeing. There were at least half a dozen people loitering around the entrance, yet they all seemed to be totally ignoring a scruffy young lad who was systematically stockpiling a growing number of toys that were being handed out to him through the half-opened window of the children's waiting room. His inside accomplice was obviously not very tall because all that I could see were a few brown curls, and the hand which emerged now and then was hardly bigger than a toddler's. The boy outside was himself only about nine or ten years of age and the more I looked at him the more convinced I became that I had seen him somewhere before. In fact, I was sure of it, but couldn't quite remember where from.

The first thing I couldn't help noticing was that, despite the temperature, this child was dressed in filthy, grey, short trousers and grubby ankle socks, his legs were blue with cold and caked in dirt. On his feet he wore ill-fitting old shoes, bereft of laces, which slip-slapped as he moved around. His bright green, quilted anorak looked paper-thin and was covered in dozens of frayed holes, many of which looked distinctly like cigarette burns. The poor kid must have been almost hypothermic with cold.

I edged my way slowly towards the boy in order not to alert him to my presence and, as I got closer, I could clearly see a whole heap of swag collected at his feet ready to be spirited away. I was almost within grabbing distance of this lad's collar when, somehow sensing my approach, he suddenly shot off down the road like a bat out of hell. It was futile for me to contemplate chasing after him and, seeing the speed at which he was shifting, I think even Linford Christie would have been hard pushed to catch him. Besides, I had neither the energy nor the inclination to do so and it was far too early in the night for me to be indulging in any heroics. It didn't matter, though, because in the brief moment when he turned around to face me I recognised him as Michael, one of the multiple offspring of the dreaded Barnes family. Every single member of this particular dynasty was well-known to the local police, ambulance service and casualty staff alike. The whole clan were an absolute night-mare and, according to local legend, the parents were clones of Fagin and Nancy; their numerous feral children were expected to bring home to them anything of value they might come across, whether by fair means or foul (but usually the latter), which would then be sold on, with the proceeds normally ending up over the bar in their local pub.

The 'inside man' was still nonchalantly pushing more toys out through the open window, completely unaware that his partner in crime had done a runner. By the time I reached the main entrance door, the miniature burglar had realised that he was now on his own. He rapidly abandoned his post, ran hell for leather out of the children's waiting room and bounced off my legs as he smacked into me at full speed. Momentarily winded by the impact, he collapsed to the floor with a thud, before scrambling to his feet and frantically scurrying away to the adult waiting room, to try to find some comfort from his mum. Hurling himself on to her knee with reckless abandon, he cuddled into her like the baby that he still was, a perfect pair of green candles sliding blissfully from his nostrils (as invariably seemed to be the case every time I encountered him).

This little lad, believe it or not, was barely four years old. Jack was the youngest of the Barnes children and, most alarmingly, was already adept at petty theft and swearing. I was hot on his heels and soon came face to face with his harridan of a mother and Gerard, yet another of her dubious progeny. Barbara, the matriarch of the family, initially looked startled but was instantly on the defensive and ready for trouble. I'd had numerous dealings with this woman before and rarely found her to be cooperative; more often than not, she was either drunk and/or extremely belligerent. Gerard looked very wary, making me rather suspicious as to what he might have been up to, too. Although only about ten or eleven years old, he was already completely streetwise and, tragically, I wouldn't have trusted him with anything that wasn't screwed down.

A number of the other patients, who had been dozing quietly in their boredom, suddenly became alert and pricked up their ears when they observed my hurried arrival. This sudden fracas was potentially the highlight of their evening so far and much more interesting than trying to make sense of the NHS health advice leaflets scattered about the waiting area or watching someone exsanguinate slowly in the corner of the room. A potential punch-up was far more fun so they focused-in, keen to observe the action.

I quietly and calmly regaled Mrs Barnes with the facts of her sons' recent exploits. Several pairs of ears were straining to hear what all the commotion was about and, as my little tale unfolded, there were a few outraged looks and occasional tuttings from the other patients wishing to express their disgust. I politely asked Mrs Barnes to keep a much closer eye on her children because this sort of behaviour was not tolerated in the hospital and any further problems would mean a quick telephone call to the police station. Barbara wasn't in the least bothered and simply shrugged her shoulders disinterestedly; she basically didn't give a monkey's, knowing full well that her little darlings were still under the age of criminal responsibility and no one could touch them.

By this time, the babe in arms, Jack, was quietly sobbing. In truth, he was probably more worried that he was going to get a thump from his mum for getting caught, than he was worried about my threat to call the 'Old Bill'. Poor little mite, I could only imagine what sort of childhood was in store for him; sadly, he was already poised at the top of a long slippery slope.

Mrs Barnes was a scrawny little woman in her early forties with a grimy, wrinkled face and a complete absence of teeth. Her lank, greasy hair looked like it was a total stranger to shampoo and any self-respecting head louse would have definitely thought twice before taking up squatters' rights in those filthy, matted locks. Her clothes stank of cigarettes and stale sweat, which was grossly overpowering in the confined space of the waiting room, and it was quite noticeable that the seats on either side of her were vacant, even though one or two people were still standing. She was an utter mess from head to toe, as were the rest of her family. And yet, I couldn't help but feel a certain amount of compassion for her. I dare say that she had been dragged up in the same way that she was raising her own brood. What chance would any of those children have without a role model? My own parents were also ordinary, working class people, who constantly struggled to put food on the table, but as children my sister and I were always clean and polite, and from an early age we were taught discipline and respect for other people and other people's property. It was a complete mystery to me how people could live like they were, yet in their own disjointed way this family were fiercely protective of each other, come what may.

Noticing the clock in the waiting room, I suddenly realised that it was now too late for me to have a quick cuppa before my shift started, so I made my way to the changing room and locked away my belongings. It was far from unusual for staff property to go missing and I can't forget when one of the nurses had her spare pair of shoes pinched from the staff room! When I started out in nursing a vast majority of the public held all members of the medical profession in high esteem. A doctor's word was gospel and any patient who insulted, disrespected or refused to comply with a nurse's instructions would quickly find themselves confronted by matron and left in no doubt that the consultant would be asked to arrange for their swift discharge as soon as medically acceptable. Parents, who had themselves been brought up before the National Health Service was created and previously had to pay for any medical treatments, were grateful for the service they received and usually kept strict control of their children in clinics and public areas. Discipline in general now seemed in retreat and youngsters were often allowed to run riot in Casualty without any effort whatsoever being made to control them, with other adults now reluctant to intervene. Personally, if I witness such behaviour, I never have any hesitation in taking the children back to their parent with suitable instructions as to their future conduct. Regrettably, the parents usually look at me like I have two heads whenever I suggest that they might actually try to control their own offspring. After making sure that my uniform and hair were presentable, I hurried off to report for my final shift of the year.

Chapter 2

6.00pm

Wythenshawe in south Manchester is a sprawling district of mainly local authority housing, once one of the largest overspill estates in Western Europe. Almost inevitably, such areas have developed tough, rundown pockets where unemployment, poverty and drug dealing are rife. The fictional Chatsworth estate featured in the popular Channel 4 television series *Shameless* is acknowledged to be based on Wythenshawe; the programmes are, in fact, recorded there both on the streets and in a purpose-built studio, and the hospital has been featured. Sadly, many of the characters portrayed are a little too true to life and the chaotic lifestyles of some actual residents are an undoubted embarrassment to the thousands of ordinary, decent, God-fearing families who have little choice but to be their neighbours. In complete contrast, south Manchester also has numerous wealthy suburbs and villages known as the 'Golden Triangle' of

Cheshire, beloved by multi-millionaire professional football players, wealthy businessmen and television personalities. A major airport and a comprehensive motorway network combine to ensure a steady stream of 'customers' to the hospital, which is a regional centre of excellence and major NHS resource.

The Casualty department at Wythenshawe Hospital was designed as a square within a square, with a wide corridor running around its periphery. There were two individual entrances: one at the front of the building for the walking wounded (where the reception area was located) and the other at the rear (where emergency ambulances brought in the stretcher patients). All patients, regardless of status, had to be booked in on arrival and, because computerised record keeping was relatively undeveloped at that time, the beleaguered receptionist had to gather all relevant information and record it by hand on to a casualty card. (This registered basic details including name, address, date of birth and next of kin etc., along with limited initial information about the nature of the injury or ailment.) If the patient had been brought in by ambulance and was waiting on a stretcher and was therefore unable to register personally at the desk, then an accompanying relative or friend was asked to do so for them. Otherwise, the receptionist (who usually worked solo) had to abandon her position in order to go into the treatment area to obtain the necessary information directly.

Once a patient was booked in, if they were 'walking wounded', i.e. could move around without assistance, they were asked to go to the waiting room until such time as their name was called. The time of arrival was documented on each person's casualty card and a hospital record number was allocated to ensure that, as far as possible, every patient was seen in order of their arrival. Of course, stretcher cases were treated as a priority at all times and these patients were always kept under close observation by the nurses while they were in the department. The receptionist would regularly bring the casualty cards through into the treatment area, drawing particular attention to any patients in the waiting room who, in her opinion, needed to be seen as a priority, especially any who were bleeding profusely or obviously in pain.

To say the least, the receptionist's job was demanding and often stressful; even when they weren't registering in patients they were always busy filing or searching for patient records. They also received an awful lot of aggravation, especially when people had been waiting for a long time. Being front of house, so to speak, they were always first in the firing line for any complaints. In my experience, every one of them deserved a medal for their patience and efficiency, particularly the night staff who had the additional burden of dealing with the all-too-frequent drunks. It certainly wasn't a job for the fainthearted.

I walked through the reception area where I saw Ann at

the desk already looking harassed, with at least a dozen people queuing at the window and getting restless because she kept having to break off to answer the telephone. Ann hadn't worked at the hospital for very long but was a confident and friendly middle-aged lady who was married to one of the local police officers, so she no doubt had a good idea what to expect when she took on the job.

Going through to the treatment area from reception, I looked into the first room on the left, which was the doctors' office. It had all the usual office facilities so the doctors could get some privacy to write up their patients' notes and scrutinise their x-rays, but at the moment it was empty and whoever was on duty was obviously busy elsewhere.

Past the office were the two larger examination rooms intended for stretcher cases, with the fourth and last room at the end designated as the suture room and, as such, it was kitted out with all the necessary equipment required to stitch up patients' wounds.

On the right-hand side of the treatment area stood a small refrigerator which was used to store tetanus vaccine and antibiotic injections, and directly above this was a locked wall cupboard containing the controlled drugs such as pethidine and diamorphine, which were used for severe and urgent pain relief. Only the sister or staff nurse in charge held the keys to this cupboard and, whenever any of the drugs were prescribed by the doctors, two nurses (at least one having to be fully qualified, as opposed to a student) had to check them extremely carefully and meticulously record details of the individual patient who was being prescribed the medication and the remaining stock levels in the control book. The only room on this side of the unit was the sluice, where all the disposable bedpans, urine bottles and vomit bowls were stored and subsequently disposed of in the macerator, a machine that mechanically shreds and flushes away the entire receptacle and contents after use. (This is very different from the process when I first started nursing, when all bedpans etc. were made of stainless steel and had to be emptied, washed and sterilised before re-use.) Next to the sluice were extensive wall and floor storage cupboards containing a comprehensive range of antibiotics, analgesics, creams and dressings necessary for every eventuality.

When I first started at Wythenshawe and was given a tour of the department, I was initially disoriented by the seeming maze of different rooms (my sense of direction isn't very highly developed at the best of times) and yet I quickly discovered that the layout and design actually worked very well from a practical point of view. Along the top of the square were eight rooms. The first was known as the 'overdose room' and used for any patients attending who required a stomach wash out after swallowing abnormal or potentially lethal amounts of some substance or other. All the necessary gastric lavage equipment (to use its Sunday name) was stored there and the sink was extra large in order to accommodate the voluminous jugs and bowls used during the procedure. The next six rooms were all identical to each other, in that they contained the basic chair, washbasin and a dressing trolley. (The stretchers allocated for these rooms were kept near the rear entrance of the department in a designated bay, allowing quick and easy access for the incoming emergency ambulance patients who were the people mainly examined in these rooms.) The final room at the end was the main resuscitation room (known as resus). It was a much larger double room and was used for the most urgent major cases, such as serious road traffic accidents, surgical/orthopaedic emergencies and medical emergencies, including myocardial infarctions (coronaries) and asthma attacks etc. All the emergency equipment in there was kept on standby, ready for immediate use at all times, and included: cardiac monitors and defibrillators; intravenous drips; trolleys full of pre-prepared emergency drugs; respirators with all the appropriate instruments for intubating patients unable to breathe unaided; oxygen cylinders; and suction machines. All these items were checked and double-checked at least twice a day and again after each use.

The original cardiac monitors we used when I was training many years earlier were so big they had to be moved around on a special trolley, and this trolley was so heavy you could get a hernia trying to push it. When you needed oxygen it came in industrial cylinders wheeled along by a porter, rather than being piped permanently to the bedside, and the suction machines wouldn't have looked out of place on a Dyno-Rod van. The new blood pressure monitors coming into service were automatic, the old glass mercury thermometers gradually replaced by digital sensors, stretchers were now fully adjustable and even some of the wheelchairs had been replaced by lighter, modern, collapsible models.

Completing the square of the department were eight small curtained cubicles used for the 'walking wounded', which housed most of the minor injuries. Each cubicle had its own extensive stock of dressings and dressing packs, slings, eye patches, antiseptic/saline solutions and both gauze and crêpe bandages of every size.

In the middle of all these treatment rooms were two large islands with hand-washing facilities and storage/disposal areas for both clean linen and used instruments, which were all removed daily for cleaning and replacement. Nearly everything we used in my early student days had to be cleaned and recycled. Some hypodermic syringes, for instance, were still made of glass and needed to be sterilised alongside so much other equipment in the Central Sterile Supply department (CSSD) where each day a small army of assistants cleaned and repackaged vast amounts of every-thing, from bandages to surgical instruments. Although a highly labour-intensive and old-fashioned way of working, compared to the majority of equipment nowadays, which is disposable and supplied pre-packaged for single-use, I don't ever remember hearing of any hospital-borne infections such as MRSA or C. Difficile arising because of cross contamination or lack of cleanliness.

As I made my way through the treatment area to report for duty, I glanced towards the casualty observation ward (known as cas obs) to see if it was already busy in there, too. This was an important part of the department and was used for short-term patients who may have, for example, sustained a head injury or perhaps undergone a light general anaesthetic to manipulate a broken/dislocated bone and who needed to be monitored overnight. Sometimes patients were also put into this area if they had been sent in by their GP and were waiting to be seen by one of the ward doctors for a medical or surgical problem. It was far better to put the patient here in a comfortable bed, under observation by a nurse, than to leave them lying for several hours on an uncomfortable emergency trolley which may well be needed elsewhere. At the moment there were only two patients in there, which was a good sign, but that would no doubt change as the evening progressed.

I got to the treatment area and was comforted to see that Sister Julie Barnett was working today. (Mr Ian Lee was the Nursing Officer in overall charge of Casualty, but Julie was the senior sister in charge.) She was generally considered by most nurses to be a very fair and conscientious manager, always pleasant and with a ready smile. I genuinely enjoyed working with her because she was not averse to rolling up her sleeves and helping out whenever it was busy, and neither was she afraid to get her hands dirty. Because of this she was a highly regarded member of staff.

There was a second sister on duty that evening, who I called Sister Clipboard. She was the total opposite of Sister Barnett and was one of those infuriating individuals (there is always one wherever you work) who had perfected the uncanny knack of always looking busy by simply carrying around an armful of papers, hurrying backwards and forwards but actually going nowhere and achieving very little. From day one I had become acutely aware of her regular work-avoidance tactics, which were so unlike the main body of casualty staff, who were almost entirely con-scientious and hard working. I had a black mark against my name from my first week at Wythenshawe, as far as Sister Clipboard was concerned. She was trying to pass a Ryle's tube into a patient's stomach and was unsuccessfully struggling in the attempt. I arrived on duty and the casualty officer made a pointed comment to Sister, suggesting that I have a go as perhaps I had a little more patience. I tentatively offered my help and, much to Sister's annoyance, managed to get it in first time. She took a dislike to me from that day on. I can understand that she may have felt a little embar-rassed that one of her staff nurses was able to complete a minor procedure she had been unable to accomplish herself, but I almost wish I hadn't offered to help in the first place.

A second incident happened one evening when the

department was having a rare quiet moment and I was attending to a patient in cubicle number one. The patient had sustained a rather nasty blow to the head after tripping and falling heavily against a brick wall and he had already vomited twice and was experiencing severe headaches and visual disturbance. The casualty officer had examined him carefully and was in the process of attempting to ascertain exactly how he had sustained his injury and whether he had lost consciousness. Unfortunately, this doctor couldn't hear the patient's replies due to the loud conversation of two members of staff, who were chatting and laughing around the corner. After failing to hear the man's responses for a second time, the doctor angrily turned to me and asked in a rather exasperated voice if I would go and tell them to keep the noise down. I dutifully went to investigate where the voices were coming from but could only see Edna, one of the auxiliaries, having a rather lively conversation with a second person who was standing partially inside the store cupboard but behind the door, completely out of my view.

I whispered to Edna, 'Please can you keep your voices down, doctor can't hear the patient.'

Edna, who was a really friendly, approachable lady, apologised immediately. However, as I made my way back to the cubicle I heard the familiar dulcet tones of Sister Clipboard growl, 'Who the hell does she think she is, telling me what to do?'

There was nothing I could do or say at the time but my heart sank and started beating faster in anticipation of World War III. And, boy, did hostilities break out. As soon as the patient had gone for his x-rays and there was no one else waiting, I went to face the onslaught and tried to explain to Sister that it was the doctor who had asked me to speak to whoever had been creating the disturbance. I knew immediately that I was wasting my breath; she seemed to be gunning for me and this had presented her with the ideal opportunity. It clearly didn't matter a jot to her what the doctor had said, she was blazing mad and, when she finally decided she was ready to speak to me, I was virtually frogmarched into the main sisters' office.

Before I could utter a word she looked me straight in the eye and with real venom in her voice bawled, 'We don't like you in this department. You come on duty and think you are in charge. Well, you're not.'

The barrage of insults continued for what seemed like a lifetime and, much to my disgust, I felt myself filling up, although more in anger and frustration than because of any hurt feelings. I desperately didn't want her to have the satisfaction of seeing me upset but, no matter how hard I tried, I couldn't hold back the tears. I made up my mind from that minute on that I would just have to avoid her like the plague and only speak to her when it was absolutely necessary; after all, I loved my job and had absolutely no intention of letting her drive me away. I was determined that I was not going to lose any sleep because of her unwarranted attack.

I cringed inwardly when I saw her standing there on New Year's Eve but purposely put on my best smile and wished both Sister Barnett and Sister Clipboard a gushing, 'Good evening.' Sister Barnett beamed and responded in kind. Sister Clipboard remained resolutely grim and silent. It could turn out to be a long night.

Chapter 3

6.05pm

I hurried over to the minor injuries area where I was due to work alongside Eileen, who I saw was on her own and rushing around trying to do six jobs at the same time. Eileen, a quietly spoken staff nurse, was tall with raven-black hair. In her mid-forties and happily married with grown-up children, she had worked part-time in Casualty for many years and knew the department like the back of her hand. Always calm, cool and collected, nothing ever seemed to bother her. Somewhat unbelievably, and in spite of the constant stream of innuendo and ribald comments which seemed to be the politically incorrect everyday feature of casualty life, she was also incredibly innocent and naïve. She frequently caused the younger nurses to roar with laughter or shake their heads in despair when they found themselves having to explain a patient's saucy remark or risqué joke. I had quickly become very fond of Eileen and was always pleased when I was rostered to work with her because she reminded me so much of myself when I first started out on my nursing career. Coming fresh from a Catholic girls' school, where for some reason the old nun in charge didn't really see sex education or human biology as a high priority on the curriculum, I found myself suitably embarrassed one day when, as a young cadet, I dutifully obeyed a request to go along to the main general operating theatre at Blackburn Royal Infirmary to borrow a packet of female fallopian tubes. The pitying look on the charge nurse's face haunted me for years.

Tonight there were two other trained nurses on duty in the treatment area on day shift: a part-time staff nurse called Valerie, who was originally from Northern Ireland and who, like Eileen, had worked in the department for several years; and George, a senior State Enrolled Nurse [SEN], who was a friendly, hard-working and very capable young man. (Staff nurses trained as students and undertook three years of both practical and theoretical instruction to attain the State Registered Nurse [SRN] qualification, from which they were able to progress to a ward sister's post and beyond; while enrolled nurses were regarded as pupils rather than students but, just like students, attended lectures part-time and worked on the wards. Their training lasted two years and enabled them to attain the SEN qualification.) Val and George were working over on the stretcher side and, at the time, they, too, were both extremely busy.

There was also one student nurse on duty, Sally, who was in her final year of training and sadly didn't enjoy working in Casualty. Personally, I think it is a department that you either love or hate, because it is so different to the rest of the hospital. Her main grumble, though, was that she felt the permanent staff had their own little clique and wouldn't let anyone else in. She confided to me one day that, unless another student was also on duty, no one spoke to her unless it was to tell her what to do. I could understand exactly how she felt and tried to reassure her that the staff considered her to be a very capable nurse, the problem was simply that everyone was generally so busy; but she was very unhappy and simply counting the days until she could leave.

It was easy for me to understand what she was going through though, because in any specialised unit, such as casualty or theatre, the permanent staff work closely together as a highly skilled team, and when I was a student myself I sometimes found it difficult to fit in if I was only going to be there for three months. No matter how friendly and accommodating the existing staff were, they had their well-established friendships and sometimes students were unintentionally left adrift. Sally was looking after the two patients in the observation ward and, because she was not yet qualified, she was being carefully supported and monitored by Sister Barnett, who kept popping in and out to confirm that she was coping (which she invariably was).

Finally, there was an auxiliary nurse called Rita, a short, bespectacled, jolly lady with lots of experience in Casualty, who was generally called to help out wherever an extra pair of hands was needed.

Eileen was up to her eyes in it and greeted me with a relieved smile. Although she was normally one of the most even tempered and laid back people I had ever met, poor Eileen seemed unusually stressed and working alone she was clearly struggling to get through the high volume of patients because of constant interruptions. Several different telephones were insistently demanding attention and she was also fielding a number of enquiries being put to her by the receptionist. The first two patients had been sent off to X-ray and Eileen was busy applying a crêpe bandage to the leg of a third. After completing this task, she gave me a brief update on the other patients waiting for treatment before washing her hands and promptly disappearing back into the next cubicle. Without further ado, I donned a very fetching white plastic apron, scrubbed my own hands and went in to the next patient who was sitting quietly waiting for attention.

While Eileen made her way down the line of cubicles, one of the casualty doctors, Dr Davies, was doing the same, leaving written instructions of the treatments he required for each individual patient. Goodness knows how many times he must already have done this since 9.00 that morning. There were always four doctors covering each twenty-four-hour shift. Senior house officers (SHO) were usually young men and women who had only just completed their first year since qualifying as a doctor, and most of them were overawed by the responsibility when they first started their six-month rotation in Casualty. At that time there were no consultants or registrars who based themselves perm- anently in the department, and certainly not on nights, so these young doctors really had to be on their mettle when it came to diagnosing the problem. All hospital Casualty departments have slightly different ways of working, too, so they usually came to rely quite heavily on the support of the senior nurses to guide them until they were confident with the protocols. Consultants from the orthopaedic wards were especially notorious because they each varied widely in the way they treated certain fractures. Some doctors stuck to tried-and-tested, old-fashioned methods, while others were far more innovative. Until the new doctors and nurses became familiar with each consultant's preferences, the permanent staff tried to guide them in the right direction.

When first starting at Wythenshawe, I was treating a patient who had punched someone else and fractured a couple of metacarpals (the bones in his own hand). The doctor who had examined and x-rayed him was also new and he asked me to carry out a specific treatment, which was then known as a boxing glove splint. I had applied this method of strapping umpteen times before at other hospitals and never gave it a second thought. It entailed getting the patient to grip a small gauze bandage, thus forming a clenched fist with the injured hand. Next, using narrow Elastoplast strapping and starting at the wrist, individual strips were run down the back of the hand and each individual finger (missing out the thumb) and over the fist before returning to the underside of the wrist. All the ends of the strips were then taped over to prevent them from coming off. This splinted the fingers in pretty much the way a boxer's hands are bandaged prior to a fight, keeping them fixed while allowing the bones opportunity to rest and heal (although, if the fractures are more serious, an operation is usually required).

The following morning, the new doctor and I were both admonished by the orthopaedic consultant who, according to Sister Barnett, had apparently gone ballistic when he examined the patient in clinic because Wythenshawe didn't use that particular method any more. We took our tongue lashing with great respect and soon learnt to check everything until we were absolutely certain that we were current.

The team of doctors on duty that New Year's Eve had already been working in Casualty for about four months though, so they were familiar with all the daily routines and procedures, and were proving to be both efficient and hard working.

I looked across to the stretcher side and saw that Dr Burn and Dr Pickering were busy seeing patients there. That meant the missing fourth casualty officer, Dr Cross, had drawn the short straw and was going to be covering the night shift all on his own.

Before I even had the opportunity to say hello to my first patient, who was a frail old lady with a dowager hump (a deformed upper spine commonly due to osteoporosis), she whispered to me conspiratorially that, as soon as Eileen had been called away, she had observed a scruffy youth sneak into the treatment room area from the waiting room and start rummaging around in the box of casualty cards before blatantly moving one of the cards from the back of the pile to the front. When she challenged him she received a mouthful of obscene abuse. I had no doubt whatsoever who was responsible for this little bit of espionage; it had to be Gerard, the other young member of the Barnes' clan! Deep down I was actually quite impressed; I didn't think he could read. When I checked, sure enough, Jack Barnes's name had been put at the front of the pile, although his time of arrival and allocated casualty number did not correspond with the others, so I returned it to the box in the correct order. I have to admit it was quite tempting to get him seen as soon as possible, if only to get rid of this troublesome family, but that would inevitably and quite rightly have caused uproar from all the other people who were sitting waiting patiently for their turn, plus I didn't want to let them get away with such a sneaky little trick.

The elderly lady who had snitched (who was well into her eighties) waited patiently, chatting away to me quite happily about her own great-grandchildren and emphasising just how polite they were and what good manners they possessed, while I checked her casualty card to see what treatments the doctor had recommended for her fairly minor but clearly painful grazes she had sustained to her hands after falling on the garden path at home. Eileen had already cleaned off the deeply embedded dirt and gravel prior to the doctor examining her without needing to use local anaesthetic and, having already established that no bones were broken, all that was needed was a simple antiseptic dressing on both hands. Dr Davies had also suggested that her tetanus status be checked and, if necessary, she be offered a tetanus booster because the wounds had been particularly dirty and full of soil. The dressings only took a minute or two to complete and the lady didn't so much as bat an eyelid, even though it must have been a little uncomfortable, but when I told her that the doctor had recommended a tetanus booster her face changed colour; you would have thought that I had asked her to hand over her purse.

In a matter of seconds, she changed from a sweet little old lady to the devil incarnate and she struggled to her feet screeching, 'You're not giving me one of those. You can stick it up your arse!'

I didn't know whether to laugh or cry and for a second or two was completely at a loss as to what to say. Where on earth had that come from? In the end, I couldn't help but laugh out loud (as did half the other patients who were sat waiting in the cubicles listening to this mini tantrum), but she was relentless in her determination to keep me as far away from her as possible, even though I hadn't so much as attempted to get the syringe out of the cupboard. She was waving her arms around like a whirling dervish and I realised that there was no chance on this earth I was going to persuade her to have the injection, despite patiently trying to explain why the tetanus vaccine was potentially so important. I was fairly certain that, having survived successfully to the grand old age of eighty-four, she would more than likely have built up her own natural immunity against tetanus but, just to be on the safe side, if she wasn't going to have a booster, I advised her to keep a close eye on the wounds in case of infection and to return to Casualty or see her GP if she was worried.

In the end, I simply had to accept there was nothing more I could do. After getting her to sign a form to confirm that treatment had been refused, she shuffled off into the night, accompanied by her seventy-year-old sister, still muttering and cursing under her breath.

Eileen and I cleared the rest of the cubicles in record time, as none of them needed a great deal of treatment. The two who had been sent to X-ray both now returned clutching their films for the doctor to check, so Eileen put them in the first two cubicles so they would be seen first, before bringing in the next six from the waiting room. As we settled each one into their respective cubicles, cleaned their wounds and checked their injuries, the doctor once again worked his way methodically down the line.

Eileen went in to see the first patient who had returned from X-ray. The doctor had diagnosed a Colles' fracture (broken wrist), so Eileen disappeared into the plaster room with the patient to put on a cast, leaving me to carry on with the other seven. Just as I started wading my way through the doctor's instructions, out of the corner of my eye I noticed Mrs Barnes sidle into the treatment area to peek at the box of casualty cards. Like all the regulars, she was fully aware how the system worked and, even though the cards were filed away from general view, with a couple of nurses in close proximity to keep an eye on them most of the time, she took her chance and knew exactly where to find them. She was probably wondering why Jack's name had not been called with the last group to come through. When she couldn't see her precious offspring's name near the front of the box, she looked quite put out and brusquely demanded to know how much longer the little darling was expected to wait.

'I'm afraid he will have to wait his turn like everyone else,' I said firmly, and made it clear that we knew 'someone' had been seen interfering with the cards. She stormed back to the waiting room, effing and blinding under her breath.

★

Next in line was an eight-year-old called Steven. He had been sitting quietly with his mum, who by now was looking thoroughly fed up, holding on to his 'sore' arm very dramatically. After a quick look at his card I smiled and asked, 'Now then, Steven, what have you done?'

I noticed the doctor had a big grin on his face as he moved between cubicles, casting his eyes heavenwards before giving me a big wink. On the boy's casualty card Dr Davies had suggested using a strong magnifying glass in order to find the 'wound' and proposed we check his tetanus status to make sure he was up to date. Nothing else had been written on the card apart from several very large question marks.

'I've got a new kitten and it's scratched my arm,' he replied, looking particularly sorry for himself.

'Let me have a look at it then, sweetheart, and I'll clean it up for you.'

He rolled his sleeve up to the elbow to show me his arm, but I couldn't see a scratch anywhere.

'Where is it?' I asked, 'Can you show me where it is, please?'

'Don't know,' he said, frantically hunting for the elusive scratch that seemed to have miraculously healed itself and evaporated into thin air.

'Wasn't it on your other arm?' his mum suggested, trying unsuccessfully to keep the frustration out of her voice. Up went the other sleeve and, after an exhaustive search, we identified the tiniest scratch that had barely broken the surface of the skin. I tentatively asked his mum if Steven was up to date with his tetanus vaccines.

'No,' she spat out in disgust. 'I don't believe in vaccinations. None of my kids have had them and I'm not going to start now!'

I was a little taken aback by her attitude. Although there have always been a small minority of parents who were never vaccinated themselves and therefore see no reason to protect their own children, whether that might be through fear, ignorance or a misguided desire to protect them, I wasn't sure why she had come to Casualty in the first place if that was how she felt. Taking a deep breath I ventured, 'Please don't get upset. We won't do anything that you don't want us to. Doctor just wanted me to ask the question. But if you don't want vaccinations, and there isn't much of a scratch to see or clean up, is there anything else you are worried about?'

She looked at me like I was completely crackers and then, out of the blue and without any preamble whatsoever, she shouted at the top of her voice, 'Call yourself a nurse? Are you stupid? Have you not heard of rabies? I want him to have treatment in case he gets rabies.'

A barely contained titter came from the adjoining cubicle and, out of the corner of my eye, I observed a middle-aged man with his large fist clamped across his mouth trying to stifle his laughter. Doing my best to ignore him and to keep my own composure, I asked, 'Have you been abroad recently where your son has been bitten by an animal?'

'What the f**k are you talking about? We can't afford to go abroad.'

I had to be careful how to proceed with this; she was obviously worried and I didn't want to antagonise her further.

'Well, the thing is, we don't have rabies in this country and, unless he has been bitten by a rabid animal somewhere abroad, there is very little chance of him getting the disease. And, besides which, as part of the treatment for rabies he would need to have a course of vaccinations.'

Apart from further muffled laughter in the next cubicle, you could have heard a pin drop. Suddenly, after refusing to sign a disclaimer, the little lad's mum leapt to her feet, gave him a clip round the ear and screamed, 'You stupid little bugger. I've been sitting in that bloody waiting room for over two hours because of you. You and your bloody rabies; get home and keep out of my sight.'

The poor child looked totally bewildered and wandered out with his head lowered and his hands shoved deep inside his pockets, feet scraping dejectedly along the floor, followed closely by an angry mother pushing and shoving him at every step. I took stock for a moment or so, trying hard not to laugh out loud but, by this time, the bloke in the next cubicle couldn't contain himself any longer and was nearly wetting himself. I bit my lip and smiled at him as I tried my very best to look as professional as possible, without making any revealing comment as to my true feelings.

Good grief, this hadn't been a particularly promising start to my shift; I had only seen a few patients and already two of them had sworn at me. I could only hope that my evening would improve.

The giggling individual in the neighbouring cubicle was next.

'Bloody hell,' he laughed, shaking his head. 'We get them like that all the time in my job.'

It turned out that he was a policeman and had been assaulted earlier in the day while trying to arrest an offender. His wrist was bruised, painful and slightly swollen so, as a precaution, his sergeant had sent him along to have it checked out. (Of course, the worse the injury, the more serious the criminal charge to be brought against the perpetrator.) As it turned out, the injury was nothing more debilitating than a mild contusion and it only required a cold compress, a smearing of Lasonil to reduce the bruising, a crêpe bandage and elevation in a sling; so I had him on his way in a few minutes.

'Have a good new year when it comes,' he shouted as he left the unit, still with a broad grin on his face. 'I hope you aren't too busy tonight.'

'You, too,' I smiled back. 'And don't you be sending us all your drunks either.'

I saw Eileen return with her tights and shoes now liberally

spattered with plaster of Paris. As she was trying unsuccessfully to wash it all off in the sink, Ann, the receptionist, came towards us looking rather miffed. A young man called Ryan, aged about thirty, had declined to answer any of her questions other than to give his name and address. He had flatly refused to say what the problem was. There was precious little privacy at the reception desk and he had (quite understandably in hindsight) no desire to inform half of Wythenshawe about his personal medical details, but had implored Ann to allow him to speak to a nurse or doctor in private as a matter of great urgency.

As Eileen was otherwise engaged chipping white gunge from her shoes, I volunteered to go and see what was wrong. To be honest, I went out fully expecting to see someone who was simply trying to pull a fast one and jump the queue (as this was commonplace), but it took me only seconds to pick out which patient she was talking about. The young man was leaning against the wall clutching the front of his jeans and looking desperately unhappy. Fighting back tears, yet at the same time apologising for being a nuisance, he could barely stand up or speak because of his obvious pain. Not wanting to cause the poor lad any further embarrassment by asking him any intimate questions out there in the public area, I asked the nurses working on the stretcher side if I could use their end room for a situation requiring a little more privacy. We left Ryan's friend, who had accompanied him to the hospital, to fill in the rest of the casualty card as best he could. Several patients waiting in line at the desk, who had overheard Ryan begging to be seen, began to whinge loudly about the injustice of it all, especially now that he was queue-jumping. Having heard it all before, I let them grumble on until I had investigated; if the injury was not genuine then he would have to return to the back of the queue and wait like everyone else.

After catching his breath, Ryan explained that he had been out playing squash with his best mate at the local sports centre. After their game he had gone to take his usual shower but, after drying himself, realised that he had forgotten to take a spare pair of clean underpants with him. Not wanting to put the sweaty originals back on, in his wisdom he decided to go commando until he got home. Big mistake! While he was busily chatting to his friend and not paying the attention such a potentially delicate situation demands, he rather incautiously zipped up his jeans and caught the skin of his penis in the metal teeth of the zip. At this point he released his grip on the front of his jeans to show me the evidence. I can honestly say that my eyes watered in sympathy to see several little pink buds of skin pushing out through the fully closed zip. Three inches of prime flesh were well and truly enmeshed.

'Oooh!' I cringed in sympathy, not quite sure where to start. My first thought was to cut the zip out of his jeans so that at least the weight of the material wouldn't drag on his skin. 'Can you manage to get on to the stretcher so that I can see more clearly?' I asked, but this proved so agonising as to be impossible for him. There was nothing for it, I had to kneel down in front of him and, very carefully, wearing latex gloves and using round-ended scissors, cut around the perimeter of the zip. Now, I have to confess I felt a tiny bit embarrassed doing this; after all, we were of a similar age and I didn't know the bloke from Adam, yet here I was on my knees delving down the front of his trousers.

Trying to break the tension in the room, I looked up into his eyes and said, 'I hope nobody walks in now, they'll wonder what on earth I'm doing!'

He blushed to the roots of his hair and started to laugh, but immediately had to stop when he doubled up in agony, 'Please don't make me laugh it hurts too much.'

It took me several more minutes to complete my mission successfully and it did seem to afford him some slight relief. He was well and truly stuck, though, and I strongly suspected that he would need to be given a light general anaesthetic (rather like the anaesthetic a dentist would administer; short, but powerful enough to knock the patient out briefly) in order to release him from his predicament.

Now that he could move a little easier, I helped him on to the stretcher, covered him up with a blanket and went to find a doctor with warm and gentle hands. As I was about to leave the room, he shouted, 'Please will you ring my wife? I should have been home for tea by now, she will be worried.'

'Will do,' I replied, and off I went.

Both Dr Davies and Dr Burn were available and when I described this young man's predicament they each squirmed before going in to inspect the damage and decide how to proceed. In the meantime, I acquired the telephone number from his friend and went to ring the wife.

It is always tricky ringing a patient's relatives because as soon as the word hospital or Casualty is mentioned people tend to panic. It is important, therefore, not to frighten them and to choose your words carefully. In an unusual situation like this one, it is also important not to make inappropriate remarks that may offend. As soon as his wife answered the telephone, I kept my voice light and said, 'Hi. Is that Mrs Stubbs?'

'Yes it is. Who's this please?'

Without answering her immediate question, I went on to say, 'Ryan has asked me to give you a ring to let you know that he is going to be a little late home.' (Hopefully this immediately conveyed to her that he was OK, because he had asked me to ring her.)

'Why? Where is he? Is he OK?'

'He's absolutely fine but he has got himself into a rather awkward and embarrassing predicament, which he is trying to sort out at present.' I then went on to tell her what had happened and that at this precise moment he was being seen in Casualty by the doctor. Initially she went very quiet, then after contemplating the scenario for a few more moments she started to giggle uncontrollably, before becoming almost hysterical with laughter.

'I don't think he's laughing at the moment, poor lad, and I can guarantee you one hundred per cent that he is unlikely ever to do this again!'

'What's going to happen to him?' she asked, trying hard to catch her breath.

'I'm not sure yet. There are several options, but if these don't work he may have to be given a general anaesthetic in order for the doctors to release him. Try not to worry; the doctor will have him sorted out soon.'

Again there was silence. But she must have begun to think about it and asked if it was OK to come and see him.

'Of course it is. In fact, I think he would appreciate it. But please try to contain yourself because if you laugh too much you'll be dead meat!'

Still giggling at the thought, she said she would come as soon as she could and then hung up.

I immediately went to tell Ryan that his wife was on her way and learnt that the casualty officer had found it necessary to call in the surgeons. KY jelly and local anaesthetics weren't options in this case, so it looked as though he was going to have to have a general anaesthetic after all. Luckily he hadn't had much to eat or drink since mid-morning, so by the time his wife arrived he was being moved into a surgical ward to be prepared for theatre.

Later that evening, we were told by the on-call surgeon

that they had gone through a really difficult time trying to release him without causing further, perhaps even permanent, damage. He was eventually freed successfully by unpicking the zip one tooth at a time, which left him with a rather bruised and lacerated pride and joy.

After Ryan left the department it was back to the cubicles where I once again found myself face to face with the delightful Mrs Barnes and Jack, who was bouncing up and down on her knee as he waited for the doctor. His nasal secretions were still totally out of control and when a good sniff failed to vacuum them upwards, both sleeves came in remarkably handy. A box of tissues was proffered and left close by, but my suggestion that he should actually use them was ignored completely by his mum, who continued to glare at me. There was no sign of the two older boys, which was a concern, but we were too busy for me to waste much time worrying where they were or what they might be getting up to.

When it was Jack's turn, the doctor asked Mrs Barnes what was wrong with him.

'He's got this bastard snotty nose all the time,' she said, pointing to the candles, 'and a sore throat.'

'Have you tried giving him anything from the chemist?'

'No.'

'Why not?'

'Because I'm on f**king benefits and can't afford to pay

cash. I need a prescription. Besides, it's easier to come here.'

'Have you seen your family doctor?'

'No.'

'Why not?'

'Because I can't stand him.'

Dr Davies was a tall, thin man with short mousey hair and a clean-shaven complexion. A very efficient, hard-working doctor, he was a real gentleman and a lay-preacher, but in the last few months he had not quite hardened to the Wythenshawe regulars' bad language and personal hygiene problems. Aged in his early thirties, he was married but didn't, as yet, have any children of his own and, while trying his utmost to be patient with Mrs Barnes, he quietly advised her through gritted teeth, 'You really mustn't come to Casualty for things like this; we have enough to do dealing with emergencies.'

The minor injuries section of any Casualty is intended to provide a service solely for the 'walking wounded', but it never ceased to amaze me how the public regularly used it as an extension of their local GP surgery, often turning up with the simplest of ailments that could and should have been treated by their own family doctor or a local pharmacist. Conversely, people thought nothing of traipsing along to Casualty and sitting for hours on end in a stuffy, germ-ridden waiting room in the expectation we would give them some magic antibiotic that would miraculously cure the virus causing their runny nose, despite their GP having already (quite correctly) refused to prescribe anything because viruses don't in fact respond to antibiotics. Others suddenly decided at 1.30am that their haemorrhoids urgently required treatment or the unsightly mole on their nose needed to be removed that minute. You'd think that people would have something better to do with their time, especially on New Year's Eve.

Dr Davies examined Jack reluctantly, checking his ears, nose and throat, before asking me what the child's temperature was (it was only slightly raised), and he chatted away amiably to the little lad to inquire how he felt. Jack didn't want to answer any of the questions put to him; he simply turned away and ignored the doctor completely, cuddling tightly into his mum's arms instead.

After completing his examination, Dr Davies looked at Barbara and said, 'Your son has got a virus so he doesn't need antibiotics. I will give him some Calpol this time to ease his discomfort and keep his temperature down but next time, go to your GP. If you don't like your GP then I suggest you find yourself another one.'

'We've been to all the other doctors and they are all f**king useless bastards,' Mrs Barnes replied.

The conversation came to an abrupt end at this point as the doctor walked away shaking his head in disgust.

'He's a miserable bastard 'n' all,' she sniffed, looking at me and nodding in the doctor's general direction, before snatching a bottle of Calpol from me and waltzing out, dragging Jack along behind her.

When I was growing up, if my parents couldn't afford to buy medicines from the chemist then they had to go to the local doctor and pay him a small fee, or do without. Nowadays, of course, the National Health Service ensures that all children, anyone on a low income, the unemployed and the elderly are all entitled to free prescriptions. Consequently, as long as people are given free medicines, they tend to go to wherever is most convenient for them and expect/demand immediate attention.

Of course, the main problem always was, and still is, lack of education. What some people genuinely consider a dire emergency is often nothing more than a simple, easy to remedy, everyday ailment. Unfortunately, few people understand basic first aid or the treatment of minor health problems so they can't really be blamed for not knowing what to do for the best when they are confronted by ill health. One GP recently reported that his most memorable 'emergency' call was from a patient who had been bitten by a dog while on holiday and had been given a tetanus injection in a Spanish hospital. They advised the lady to inform her GP about what had happened immediately on her return to England. She took them at their word and rang him as soon as she reached home. It was 3.00am on a Sunday morning!

There are now GPs and practice nurses, NHS direct

telephone advice services, school nurses and walk-in centres providing round-the-clock advice and first aid; while organizations like the St John's Ambulance Brigade and The Red Cross put on first aid classes everywhere. Perhaps if every school included this type of information as part of their curriculum, it would reduce many unnecessary future visits to Casualty.

Chapter 4

7.00pm

Sister Barnett was helping out on the stretcher side when she took an urgent call from ambulance control alerting staff that two potentially serious cases were about to descend on Casualty. This advance warning had the nurses running around, moving existing patients out of resus in readiness to accommodate the more potentially demanding admissions.

Ambulance control always tried their best to give us plenty of notice with any pending emergency, as this gave the nurses time to prepare the appropriate equipment and allowed the doctors to get themselves psyched up, ready for the challenge. Both patients were deemed to be a priority so, as there were already a number of stretcher patients needing the attention of the nurses working in that area, Sister shouted that Eileen and I should leave what we were doing in minor injuries in order to help her. We quickly apologised to the patients in the cubicles and said that we were going to have to abandon them. They were already switched on to the heightened activity levels and had overheard our conversations so knew they were going to have to wait, but at least they now had the prospect of a little action to relieve the boredom.

Minutes later, the unmistakable dual-tone emergency sirens could be heard heading in our direction; the blue flashing lights of two ambulances reflected in the cold night air as they hurtled around the corner towards the hospital at high speed, closely followed by an accompanying police traffic car. Adrenaline was now kicking in pretty rapidly. In anticipation of what was to come, Dr Pickering and Dr Burn, the two casualty officers working on the stretcher side, together with several of the nursing staff (including Eileen and myself), hurried to the rear entrance with stretchers ready to meet the ambulances. Within seconds of their arrival, two teams were haring back down the corridor to resus, each with their own individual patient, as our carefully choreographed and well-rehearsed procedures sprang into operation.

Although these two patients arrived simultaneously, they were in no way connected. The first and most serious of the two emergencies was a critically injured young man, aged about thirty who, according to the attending police officer, had been driving home from work along the motorway when the front tyre on a large articulated lorry suffered a blowout. Losing control and swerving violently across all three lanes of traffic, the lorry clipped several vehicles before sending our patient's car into a spin, which in turn sent him crashing into other cars and causing an even bigger multiple pile-up. Unbelievably no other people were reported to be seriously injured. Our patient's identity had been quickly established at the scene of the accident by the traffic police through his vehicle registration details and the officer accompanying the victim informed us that one of his colleagues had been sent to contact the patient's relatives. Documents and photographs found in the car and in his wallet seemed to indicate that the man was married with two very young children.

The patient's name was Stuart and on admission he was drifting in and out of consciousness, but he looked desperately ill. He was immediately put on oxygen while Sister and I started to undress him as quickly and as carefully as we could, trying to ensure that we didn't make his injuries any worse or cause him any further undue pain. As usual in any serious case such as this, speed was of the essence, so any clothing that couldn't be removed easily was unceremoniously cut off with scissors.

(I had been involved with one particular case, several months previously, where a middle-aged businessman had been rushed into Casualty after going into cardiac arrest in the back of the ambulance. Unable to get his clothes off quickly enough to give him urgent necessary treatment, we had cut them off. The patient was successfully resuscitated before being admitted to the coronary care unit and after two weeks in there he eventually went home. At that point, he wrote a vitriolic letter of complaint and put in an insurance claim to the hospital because the careless staff in Casualty had destroyed his best suit!)

Dr Burn took charge of Stuart and hovered alongside the stretcher carefully checking each area of the patient's body as his clothes were removed. As soon as he was able to assess what was needed, he began taking a series of blood samples ready to go to the laboratory for urgent checks; these would include a full blood count, biochemical profile, blood sugar, grouping and cross-matching. These tests were all carried out as a matter of routine and would give us a clearer picture of the seriousness of Stuart's condition, as well as establishing his blood group, which would also then allow several units of blood to be put on standby in case a transfusion was necessary. Eileen helped to complete all the necessary documentation and specimen tubes before ringing for a porter to rush them to the laboratory. In the meantime, I was checking Stuart's general observations, which included consciousness level, pupil reactions, temperature, blood pressure and pulse. An intravenous saline drip was put in to keep the veins patent (open), in case he needed to be given urgent drugs or a transfusion, and a urinary catheter was inserted into his bladder in order to keep a close eye on his kidney function. At the same time as all this activity was going on, Dr Burn gave instructions for one of us to contact the radiographer and arrange for a series of urgent portable x-rays to be carried out in resus, while he contacted the on-call surgeons to inform them of Stuart's critical condition and to ask them to attend as soon as possible.

At the time, the surgeons were already in theatre busy dealing with a previous emergency and were unable to come down immediately, but the surgical houseman (the most junior doctor in surgical rotation) came to the phone, took the appropriate details and promised faithfully to pass the information on to his superior.

The patient groaned in discomfort as Dr Burn carried out all these necessary procedures, which in a strange way was heartening to hear as it meant that he was not deeply unconscious because he could still feel discomfort. However, he was grey and felt freezing cold and very clammy, which was not a good sign and indicated that he was in severe shock and more than likely bleeding internally. In particular, his breathing was shallow and laboured and giving us great cause for concern. A cardiac monitor was attached to Stuart's chest so that we could see at a glance how his heart was behaving. Oddly, there appeared to be few visible signs of injury other than two almost identical, small puncture wounds, each no bigger than the size of a ten pence piece, one on the right side of his chest and the other on the left side of Stuart's abdomen near his waist; both were literally gushing blood. Eileen and I covered these wounds temporarily with thick pads of sterile gauze and applied a firm pressure to try to stem the immediate flow, but as the intravenous drip rate was increased, more and more bloody fluid poured out. Before too long our feet and legs were gruesomely splashed with warm, red, rapidly coagulating blood and nothing we attempted was able to stop it.

Being aware that the patient was having difficulty breathing, I asked the doctor if I should set up a trolley for a chest drain (a flexible plastic tube that is inserted through the side of the chest) just in case it may be needed. He nodded and said there was a distinct possibility that Stuart had either sustained a pneumothorax or a haemothorax (a collection of air, or blood, between the lung and chest wall usually caused by a sudden trauma), but only an x-ray would show the extent of the damage. While we waited for the radiographer to arrive, Eileen and I quickly set up the trolley for the drain and Sister began to speak reassuringly to Stuart, letting him know that he was in good hands and that his wife was on her way. Patients suffering serious injuries often confirmed weeks later, during their recovery, that even though they had been unable to communicate or respond in any way at the time of their admission, they were comforted by unknown voices explaining what was about to happen to them and telling them that they were going to be OK.

Regrettably, Eileen and I felt we were probably just going through the motions; neither of us was happy with his appearance and we feared his injuries were more than likely to prove fatal.

The young female radiographer arrived only moments later pushing and steering her heavy, electrically powered, white portable machine as quickly as she could, and parking it alongside Stuart's stretcher. Dr Burn handed her a card detailing which particular x-rays he required and then, as per normal protocol, all the other staff briefly left the room to avoid any unnecessary exposure to radiation during the process. Each x-ray took only seconds to complete but I grabbed a lead-lined jacket to enable me to stay and assist her and also to keep an eye on Stuart at the same time. (If another patient or member of staff is present in the adjoining cubicle, only separated by a curtain, then they too have to be temporarily shielded by the use of lead jackets.)

The stretchers in Casualty had a relatively modern, built-in facility to accept x-ray plates in a drawer-like compartment underneath the patient, avoiding the need for staff to support or move him around more than necessary. As soon as the radiographer had completed the task, she literally ran back to her department to develop the films, returning within minutes, during which time the staff piled back into resus to continue taking general observations and monitoring his blood loss until we knew what we were truly dealing with. Dr Burn immediately put the developed films up on to the illuminated screens lining the back wall and it was soon clear that Stuart had suffered massive internal damage. It looked as though some object, probably a narrow strip of metal from another vehicle, had penetrated his chest and gone straight through his body piercing several major organs on the way, and that the two relatively minor-looking puncture wounds to his chest and abdomen were the entry and exit wounds. The surgical SHO arrived only seconds later and, after examining him thoroughly from head to toe, agreed with the casualty officer that Stuart needed to go to theatre as soon as was humanly possible. Before that could even be considered and he could be given an anaesthetic, though, it was paramount that his condition be stabilised or he simply wouldn't survive.

As soon as the laboratory rang to say that a supply of blood was ready, I ran to fetch the first unit and a transfusion was hurriedly commenced to try to replace some of the massive blood loss which was still continuing. I had rarely seen such heavy bleeding, except from a far more serious-looking injury. We needed to get Stuart's blood pressure up because it was dangerously low, so once the transfusion was underway his observations continued to be monitored at five-minute intervals to see if there were any signs of improvement. Every minute seemed like an hour as we all watched and waited hopefully for some indication of change; anything to show us that he was responding, but nothing was happening. His pulse was virtually non-existent and his blood pressure was now so low that he was in danger of cardiac arrest. Within such a short time since his admission, this poor soul was slipping into a deeply unconscious state and, mercifully at this point, he was completely oblivious to pain.

After an urgent telephone call by the junior surgeon, his senior surgical registrar (who had just finished operating only minutes before) came running into Casualty accompanied by the on-call anaesthetist. Both were still in their green theatre clothes and ready to do battle for Stuart's life.

As soon as they arrived, the anaesthetist immediately took charge; he decided not to put the chest drain in straight away, but quickly intubated Stuart (inserted a tube into his windpipe to maintain an open airway) so that a ventilator could take over his breathing and thus take the additional strain away from his heart. All eyes in the room were transfixed by the graph displayed on the screen of the heart monitor as the necessary drugs were administered. Everyone held their breath, hoping and praying that by some miracle he would survive.

The x-rays were being passed backwards and forwards between the doctors as they racked their brains and anxiously discussed what possible courses of action they could take next. The transfusion was speeded up, but all that this achieved was to make the wounds bleed even more heavily and the growing puddle of blood on the floor spread ever wider. I squeezed Stuart's hand tightly, begging him with all my heart not to leave us; urging him not to give up, even though I doubted he could still hear my words.

Over the next half hour, a long and frantic battle was fought to try to stabilise him. Theatre was put on standby but he never regained sufficient strength for the surgeons to even contemplate operating on him. In the end, all our efforts were futile and his heart began to give up the fight. As his heart stopped, cardiac massage was enthusiastically commenced with several of the team, including Sister and me, taking over from each other when one or the other became tired, and adrenaline was administered directly into his heart. But it did no good. The heart monitor continued to flatline and his pupils were fixed and dilated, indicating absolutely no sign of life. Stuart was gone.

Everyone stood there quietly for a brief moment, looking at the lifeless young body, now almost indistinguishable beneath a forest of drips, tubes and monitor wires. The anaesthetist was the first to make a move, shaking his head in despair before checking Stuart one final time and asking everyone present if they agreed that resuscitation efforts should be discontinued. In a situation like this no single doctor ever makes that final decision by himself. Every one of the doctors involved in the resuscitation attempt must agree that nothing more can be done. In this case, they all simply nodded and Stuart was duly certified dead. As the doctors dispersed, Eileen and I set about tidying up and removing all the equipment and resuscitation paraphernalia from the body. We cleaned everything that had been used and replaced everything needed to make the room ready for the next patient. Stuart was laid flat and covered completely with a sheet and then, for the sake of privacy (not really knowing whether the space in resus would be needed again at any minute), he was moved down the corridor to cas obs, where his body could at least be made more suitable for viewing by any family members who would be asked to identify the body.

As a rule, on the wards it was usual protocol to leave a body untouched for at least an hour after death before starting to lay them out. It was deemed to be not only respectful to the patient but it also gave the family a chance to come to the hospital and see their loved one before they were transferred to the mortuary. This period also afforded an opportunity for a minister of faith to attend, if requested. During nurse training it was drummed into us how essential it was to know a patient's religion (in case of serious illness or death) and this was always entered into the patient's records and/or displayed at the top of their hospital bed. Roman Catholics, for instance, often request the services of their priest, whereas only a Rabbi is permitted to touch a Jew after death. Although in the heat of the moment it may be easy to forget the necessity of such final courtesies, it is nevertheless most important that they should always be granted whenever humanly possible. Obviously patients occasionally died in Casualty without any identification on them, so until a relative or friend could be found to provide the relevant details (which could sometimes be hours or even several days later), they were usually taken to a quiet room and made presentable using the minimum amount of physical contact before eventually being sent to the mortuary. It was not feasible to keep bodies lying around in Casualty for too long because there was simply too much activity in each area. Although, if we had sufficient time, we always tried to let the relatives pay their respects before transferring the body.

Of all the really serious accidents I have seen over the years, I had never, ever seen so much blood coming from such apparently tiny wounds. It had spread everywhere and, as we rushed with the stretcher from resus to cas obs, a dark red rivulet was left behind along the full length of the corridor. We obviously didn't want anyone to see this, so had to frantically retrace our steps, trying to clean up as we went along.

As we wheeled Stuart's body into the first available room and explained the circumstances to Sally, Eileen looked down at him with great compassion and, reaching out to touch his arm, whispered, 'God bless you.'

Both of us had tears streaming down our faces as we left him there, our sympathy and thoughts now with his wife and young family.

Just as we finished mopping, a police car pulled up outside carrying a distressed-looking young woman, who we presumed to be Stuart's wife, accompanied by an older man. Eileen and I breathed a sigh of relief that we had at least managed to get rid of the most upsetting evidence of this terrible tragedy.

Sister Barnett had been watching out for their arrival and

immediately ushered them into the relatives' room, which afforded a degree of privacy before Dr Burn could join them and break the dreadful news as gently as possible. The auxiliary, Rita, who had been keeping an eye on the other stretcher patients along with Sister Clipboard, was commandeered to make a tray of tea for the relatives, which gave us a little more breathing space to make sure that Stuart's body had been made as presentable as possible and the room tidied. When everything was ready, we gave Sister the nod and she disappeared back into the relatives' room to ask the family if they were ready to see him.

When Stuart's wife entered the room he looked so peaceful that he could simply have been in a deep sleep. She, though, was in complete shock and turned white as a sheet as she tried to summon up enough courage to look at his body. Several minutes passed as she stood staring blankly at the floor before finally steeling herself. Not a word passed her lips. As she ventured a little closer and gathered the strength to gently take hold of his lifeless hand, she stared at her husband's body in pained disbelief and began shaking uncontrollably. Eileen and I didn't dare to look at each other; we were both choked up as we watched her lovingly stroke Stuart's face and brush his hair off his forehead. There were no tears as she kissed him tenderly; clearly far too traumatised and probably still in denial due to the speed of events. Instead, she remained quiet and withdrawn and my heart was breaking for her.

The policeman who accompanied her to the hospital told us later that she had two young boys at home, both under five years of age, who idolised their daddy. This tough copper also had a hint of moisture in his eyes, no doubt reflecting, as we all were, how our own families would be feeling and acting if the positions were reversed.

A post-mortem would have to be carried out, but that was for another day. Our efforts to resuscitate Stuart had gone on far longer than usual and everyone involved in trying to save his life looked totally drained, but we were confident that no one could have done more.

No matter how many times I experienced sudden tragic death, I never fully came to terms with such situations, especially when the victim was so young. While death is a great inevitability for everyone, working in a busy acute Casualty department means that you see more than your fair share of it and you simply have to accept that every patient cannot be saved. Some cases affect you more than others, though; some of us cry openly, most have a weep or a quiet moment of contemplation in private when they get home. Over the years I have seen hundreds of deaths, not all of them pleasant or peaceful, but children and young people tend to stick in my mind. One of my first cases in Casualty as a student involved a distraught mother running in and thrusting a lifeless baby into my arms, screaming for me to make him breathe. Despite every effort, the little boy couldn't be saved.

Strangely, this isn't the case that I remember most clearly over the years. The accident was entirely unremarkable; some workmen were replacing tiles on a roof and one of the younger lads started messing about and he fell to the ground. Unluckily for him, he landed on a narrow strip of concrete path; a foot or so either way and he would have landed on soft soil. Apparently, after crashing to earth he jumped to his feet, brushed himself down and said he was OK. But then he dropped down dead. He was rushed into hospital and we tried our utmost to revive him but without success. He was just seventeen years old and he didn't have a mark on his body but had broken his neck. I don't know why this particular death stays with me, other than perhaps it brought home to me for the very first time how fragile our hold on this planet is.

But, after everything, there is always another patient waiting. Before Eileen and I returned to minor injuries, we checked in on the other urgent case that had been brought in at the same time as Stuart. He was still on the other side of the curtain in resus and was being looked after by Dr Pickering, Valerie and George. Their patient was a middle-aged, heavily built man who had been admitted complaining of severe mid-sternal chest pain that radiated into his neck and down his left arm. He was in a cold, clammy sweat and looking extremely anxious. From the moment he arrived in Casualty, he insisted very loudly that there was nothing wrong with him that a good dose of milk of magnesia wouldn't cure (which he said he had been dosing himself with on and off for the last two or three days). The managing director of a large company, he was not used to being ill and quite openly admitted that he was terrified of hospitals. Any potential medical problem spooked him and, as a result, he was being less than cooperative. Having been unable to avoid hearing what was happening with Stuart on the other side of the curtain, it wasn't very surprising that he had become quite agitated and then, when he realised that Stuart had died, he'd become even worse. It was a lot for anyone to cope with, let alone someone who had been brought into a strange environment and who was feeling ill and vulnerable themselves. Unfortunately the layout of resus gave us little opportunity to prevent this kind of thing happening, and in this instance it resulted in completely unnerving the patient.

The man's name was Eric and, as far as could be ascertained, he had never previously experienced any chest pains. He hadn't been treated in hospital before, nor had he ever so much as consulted his GP. He was hopping around like a cat on hot bricks, constantly complaining that he simply didn't have the time for all this palaver and had far too much work to do; exactly how much he hoped to achieve after 7.00pm on New Year's Eve I couldn't imagine. On his arrival, Valerie had tried desperately to calm him down, and then put him on oxygen (which he persistently pulled off his face) and attached him to a heart monitor, before he was seen and examined by Dr Pickering. As soon as he had calmed down a little, a heart tracing was recorded and the doctor spoke to the radiographer (who was at the time dealing with Stuart) to request an urgent portable chest x-ray. In the meantime, as a matter of routine, a Venflon was put in a vein on the back of the patient's hand (this was a type of flexible tube used to keep a vein open, ready for the doctor to administer emergency drugs if needed) and Dr Pickering prescribed a small dose of intramuscular diamorphine to relieve his chest pain.

At this point, nothing of any significance was showing up on the heart tracing but the patient was displaying all the classic symptoms of having had a coronary and was looking decidedly grey and agitated, in addition to being soaked with sweat. Amazingly, apart from a tachycardia (a fast pulse rate, which was probably due to his barely concealed fear of hospitals, as much as anything else), there were no definitive signs of him having had a coronary, or any other type of heart problem for that matter. However, any damage to the heart (due to a coronary) that would normally be expected to show up on an ECG recording (heart tracing) may not always be immediately evident. It was set procedure, therefore, for anyone presenting with such classic symptoms to be admitted to coronary care until their blood tests and repeat heart tracing could be re-checked some hours later, when they may possibly prove conclusive.

Eric was having none of it, though, and in his wisdom considered that this was all a big fuss over nothing. What was even more alarming, he was now adamant that he wasn't prepared to stay with us any longer and intended to go home straight away. Eileen and I had overheard a lot of this conversation as we were cleaning the adjoining area after Stuart's body had been removed and genuinely felt a great deal of sympathy for this man. He was clearly scared witless of hospitals and illness in general, and couldn't even begin to accept what was happening to him. Dr Pickering, Valerie and George all tried desperately to calm him down and did their best to explain why it was essential that he should stay in hospital; they didn't want to upset him unnecessarily, but it was vital that someone spelt out the dangers to which he was exposing himself by discharging himself too soon.

Dr Pickering had already collected details of his medical history and general lifestyle from his wife when they first arrived, so he now emphasised to him that he was a high-risk candidate for heart problems. Eric acknowledged that he was in a highly stressful job, smoked forty cigarettes a day, drank a large amount of alcohol, was very overweight and rarely had time to take any exercise, that his diet was high in fat and salt and, according to him, he only slept three or four hours each night. He was a high flyer with a multi-million pound business but was living under the misconception that he was invincible and nothing could ever happen to him.

Even as he was talking to the doctor, Eric was constantly

rubbing his chest and left arm in discomfort and, although undoubtedly still in pain, he repeated that he was not prepared to lie around in a hospital bed when he had important work to do. Clearly having made up his mind, he started to disconnect his cardiac monitor and get off the stretcher. All three staff members pleaded with him once more to show some common sense. Sister Barnett, who at the time was dealing with Stuart's relatives, was sent for and requested to intervene. She pointed out very bluntly that he was putting his life at great risk and explained to Eric that he was far better spending a day or two in hospital than ending up in a wheelchair for the rest of his life. He then became quite irate and made it perfectly clear that he was not used to having people tell him what to do in such a forthright manner.

As a last desperate resort someone went to fetch his wife to see if she could make him see sense. She knew exactly what we were up against and told staff that her husband was extremely stubborn, and was used to getting his own way both at work and at home. She didn't hold out much hope of getting him to change his mind but agreed to give it a try. After tearfully begging him at least to stay in overnight, her pleas, too, were rejected. She tried to reason with him and begged him to think of her and the family, but it made not a scrap of difference. So, having categorically refused our every offer of assistance, he signed his own discharge before slowly getting dressed and shuffling down the corridor to where his wife had brought their car around to the exit. In all honesty, he looked like a dead man walking; his skin was even greyer than when he was first admitted and he was still sweating profusely.

One frustrated member of staff muttered under his breath, 'See you later, if you're lucky.' But we all still hoped and prayed that he would be OK.

Chapter 5

7.55pm

After a life-and-death emergency, it is always difficult to brush yourself down and simply carry on as though nothing had happened, but that is exactly what we had to do. Other patients were still piling up waiting to be seen and so, with a heavy heart, Eileen and I put a smile on our faces and wandered back over to the minor injuries side to pick up where we had left off. The waiting patients had been amazingly cooperative and were eager to find out what had been going on. We couldn't tell them, of course, because of patient confidentiality, although that still didn't stop them asking. Like a pair of yoyos we continued working our way up and down the line of cubicles; but that's what I loved about Casualty, one minute you were desperately attempting to save someone's life, the next you were trying to stop a nosebleed.

We carried on dealing with every manner of injury from

broken arms and legs to ingrown toenails and earache. Unbelievably, one young woman had the temerity to turn up with a broken fingernail. She had been sitting in the waiting room for well over two hours, clearly seriously concerned and most anxious to know what we proposed to do to relieve her desperate plight. Dr Davies, clearly exasperated, told her reasonably politely what she could do with her fingernail, although judging by the look on her face I don't think she was at all that impressed by his suggestion (personally, I thought he was remarkably restrained). Another young girl complained that her new ear-stud was hurting, but she was reluctant to remove it in case she couldn't get it back in again afterwards. The sheer variety of injuries and ailments was almost limitless, and far too many of them brought a wry smile of resignation to our faces because they had come to the wrong place with their trivial problems.

We tried our best to keep on top of all the treatments, so that with a bit of luck we would have them all cleared by the time the night staff came on duty. Valerie and George were dealing with a few stretcher cases brought in by ambulance, who still needed treatment, but none of them were life threatening and we were hopeful that it would stay that way. We were probably being a little too optimistic, seeing as there were going to be so many people out and about that night.

As I went out into the waiting room to call in the last few

remaining patients, I saw a couple of police officers called Ken and James at reception, trying their best to book in a very drunk man who had been found slumped against a wall in the local shopping centre. He was bleeding all over the reception area floor from a small but deep head wound and was having the utmost difficulty standing upright. Ann was completely fed up by this time; she'd had a hard day and just wanted to go home. It didn't improve her mood a great deal when the man refused to treat any of her enquiries seriously.

'What's your name?' she asked, scowling as the man swayed about like Bambi in a high wind.

'Moses,' was the muttered, barely coherent reply.

'Where do you live?'

'Mount Sinai.'

'Stop messing about,' snapped Ken. 'These people have enough to do without you wasting their time.'

Quite frankly, Ann was beyond caring, so simply began writing down everything he said verbatim.

Their little exchange was interrupted by a bright spark sitting near reception, who had been listening to the drunken repartee with great interest and who, no doubt seeing a stellar future for himself in stand-up comedy, inquired in a very loud voice, 'Has anyone seen a burning bush lately?'

Despite his all-encompassing haze of alcohol, the comment triggered Moses into a spitting frenzy of pure rage. He lunged wildly at the grinning joker and moments later an all-out rough and tumble ensued. The two officers were taken by surprise and desperately tried to separate the two men who were rolling around on the floor like a couple of children in the playground. After a minute or so, the police regained the upper hand and rapidly slapped handcuffs on Moses, at the same time warning our resident comedian to back off and keep quiet or he would be cuffed as well. As quickly as the trouble had flared, peace prevailed once more. I kept well out of the way and just let them all get on with it, while I continued shepherding my little flock through into the minor injuries section for treatment.

As I started to sort this next batch into their respective cubicles, the telephone rang and Eileen broke off to answer it. She looked increasingly puzzled as she listened to the caller and I heard her say, 'I'm really sorry, I don't know any staff nurse by that name, but I'll ask around. Just wait a minute please.' She put the receiver down before raising her voice to inquire, 'Does anyone know a Staff Nurse Timberdick?'

I nearly died. Several young male patients who were hanging about waiting for treatment started sniggering and thought either the person on the other end of the phone was having a laugh or she was; but Eileen was deadly serious. 'That would be for me,' I said, laughing, despite feeling a little embarrassed.

'But you're called Woodcock,' she said, still looking completely puzzled. It was hard to believe (but quite sweet) that she was still so innocent.

'Correct! Try to work it out quickly, Eileen, but for goodness sake keep your voice down.' She genuinely hadn't a clue how to make the connection and I wasn't going to enlighten her at that particular moment. I picked up the phone to answer the call and found that it was a local police sergeant making enquiries about an incident in the department that I'd dealt with the previous evening.

Timberdick was a nickname I had been christened with soon after I started at Wythenshawe by Wendy, one of the other staff nurses on nights, who possessed a rather wicked sense of humour. Unfortunately the name had well and truly stuck, and now seemed to be commonly used in preference to my real name by most male members of staff, the whole of Greater Manchester Police Force and quite a number of the Greater Manchester Ambulance Service crews.

Eileen was obviously still trying (unsuccessfully) to work it out as I put the police sergeant on notice that vengeance would be swift if I ever came across him as a patient, ideally while holding one of our largest hypodermic needles in my hand. He couldn't believe that she hadn't figured it out yet and was still chuckling to himself when he eventually rang off. Trying my best to avoid the subject, I busied myself with the waiting patients.

A short time after this telephone call, one of the young men waiting for treatment called me across and presented me with a pencil drawing that he had sketched while trying to pass the time. It was a cartoon of a *Carry On* type nurse in a severely abbreviated uniform, who was rather too well-endowed in the chest department to be true to life, and who sported a large name badge identifying her as 'Timberdick'. The patient was an art student at the local college and the drawing was in fact extremely professional. (I kept it for many years, but sadly mislaid it when we moved house only recently.) The humour certainly didn't pass me by and everyone who saw it thought it was brilliant.

For some reason the next patient in line had pulled the curtain across the cubicle, which was a little odd because, according to her card, she only had a nosebleed. I gave Eileen a nudge and silently mouthed to ask her why the patient had drawn the curtain. As bewildered as me, Eileen shrugged her shoulders and shook her head. Very quietly, I took a tentative peek around one side of the curtain and saw a bedraggled-looking, middle-aged woman engaged in a little bit of skulduggery. She was busily filling her coat pockets and shopping bag with bandages and dressings from the back shelves in the cubicle. The unbelievable cheek of some people really did surprise me at times! Raising my voice loud enough for the patient to hear, I asked Eileen who she wanted me to see next. She winked and loudly replied that it was the patient behind the curtain who had a nosebleed. There were frenetic scraping noises as the chair slid across the floor as the woman made a mad leap to regain her seat, and when I drew back the curtain with a flourish she was ostentatiously squeezing the end of her nose pretending to stop it bleeding. I began to peruse her casualty card carefully and, according to the recorded details, she had been experiencing heavy nosebleeds on and off all day. However, when she had been examined by the doctor a few minutes ago, there were no signs of any problem whatsoever; not even the evidence of a single spot of dried blood. Dr Davies had requested a blood pressure check (which was routine procedure because nosebleeds can sometimes indicate high blood pressure), but in this instance it was found to be perfectly normal. So, after I reported the result to him, he thought it would be pointless to pack her nose with ribbon gauze (which was the general treatment for stopping a persistent nosebleed), and instead he told me to send her home with suitable advice should there be any recurrence. As there was nothing else for me to do, at least as far as her treatment was concerned, I decided to confront the problem of her petty pilfering.

Keeping my voice as low as possible I asked, 'Can you please tell me if there was any special reason why you pulled the curtain across the cubicle?'

She looked a little flustered and appeared to be trying to dream up a half-credible excuse, before blurting out, 'I'm a bit squeamish and I didn't want to see what was going on over there, where the people are on stretchers.'

'I see,' I said, still not wanting to embarrass her in front of the other patients. 'So it wasn't because you were helping yourself to all our dressings and bandages, then?' I asked quietly. She looked absolutely mortified but, before she had the chance to dream up another little gem, I said, 'Before you leave, can you please take all the articles you have stolen out of your pockets and shopping bag and place them on top of the dressing trolley next to you?'

In that instant she became hostile and argumentative and jumped to her feet, no doubt anxious to make a rapid exit. 'I don't know what you're talking about,' she spluttered, 'Who the hell do you think you are anyway? I don't have to empty my bag for you or for anybody.'

That was certainly true enough, but after catching her in the act I had no intention of just letting her walk out. I hate dishonesty in any shape or form but, as it was New Year's Eve, I was feeling charitable enough to at least give her the chance to come clean.

'Fair enough, but let me just say this, if you don't empty them for me now I will make sure that the two policemen outside in reception know what I have seen you get up to and, make no mistake, you will be arrested and taken to the police station. It's your choice.'

She looked at me with sheer hate in her eyes and at first I thought she was going to hit me, but instead she snatched her bag and tipped the contents out on to the trolley before also reluctantly turning out her pockets. She must have been wandering around the hospital all day picking up goodies – the woman could have started her own medical supplies company with the stuff she dredged up. She was now looking completely panic-stricken at having been caught out and begged me not to tell the police. For a second or two I actually felt sorry for her, but I had seen similar performances far too many times over the years. I regarded her with both pity and disgust but reflected how desperate she must have become to be stealing bandages and sticking plasters, no doubt trying to sell them for a pittance. Deciding to exercise a degree of compassion (or would that be soft in the head?), I had a quick word with Sister, who spoke to the woman sternly and told her to get out and think herself lucky that she wasn't going to see in the new year from a police cell. The woman didn't hang around for long and scuttled out of the door, disappearing off down the road as fast as her legs would carry her. I sincerely hoped that this episode would teach her a lesson, but doubted that it would make even the slightest bit of difference. Every hospital is liable to experience a certain amount of theft simply because of the sheer size, layout and open access to the public. In the old days when visiting hours were limited it was probably a little easier to control, but such large buildings are almost impossible to secure completely. Unfortunately Wythenshawe Hospital was a particularly sprawling site with many potential candidates more than willing to exploit any opportunity or weakness.

In my opinion, security was especially lax at Wythenshawe Hospital and staff regularly left office doors unlocked with both their personal belongings and medical items lying around inside. Only when something valuable was stolen did anyone start being more careful but, even then, many hospital staff still tended to shrug their shoulders and believe that it wouldn't happen to them. This must have been extremely frustrating for the police, who had little sympathy with the complainants because they had heard it so many times before.

As I was putting all the stolen goods back on the shelves and tidying the cubicle, Ann came running in breathlessly to report that someone had been found collapsed in the ladies' toilets. Eileen and I immediately dropped what we were doing and, after once again making a hasty apology to the waiting patients (who by this time were getting totally fed up with hanging around) hurried to see if we could help.

When we reached the toilet block, the lady who had discovered and reported the prone figure was anxiously pointing to two legs protruding underneath the door of the first cubicle. We looked at each other sceptically as, even at this early stage, something didn't seem quite right. Kneeling down on all fours and looking under the gap at the bottom of the door, Eileen could see that the woman was lying flat on her back with her head tilted slightly to one side, her mouth wide open and dribbling saliva. The toilet cubicles were relatively small and yet the position that the collapsed female had somehow managed to get herself into was virtually impossible without a great deal of contrivance on her part. Her head looked rather too conveniently placed between the toilet and the cubicle wall and, in fact, she looked remarkably comfortable for someone who had supposedly been suddenly rendered unconscious. After thanking the lady who had raised the alarm for bringing it to our attention, we asked her to leave us to it.

Eileen looked at me and whispered very quietly, 'It's Margaret.'

All the permanent casualty staff knew this lady only too well and our first glimpse of the shoes should have instantly put us on alert. She was one of our most persistent regulars who always wore the same down-at-heel, flat, black shoes and an old, long, grey, fluffy coat. Just to be absolutely sure, I climbed up and stood on the adjacent washbasin so that I could peer over the top of the partition and get a better view. It was definitely Margaret who was lying on the cold hard floor like the proverbial dying swan.

All the casualty staff were thoroughly fed up with her time-wasting antics. However, Margaret suffered from a medically controversial condition known as Munchausen Syndrome, which basically meant that she feigned illness in order to gain attention. To make matters even worse, she seemed to have acquired a reasonably competent knowledge of medical jargon, which made the situation all the more precarious for our doctors because every time she came in she was able to give such a convincing detailed history of what was wrong with her that tests were usually deemed necessary to rule out the fairly remote possibility that she may, in fact, have been genuinely ill.

It is a sad fact that just about every hospital in the country is at some time plagued with these tragic individuals, who will go to extraordinary lengths to be admitted for treatment. Some go so far as to undergo unnecessary surgery, often after succeeding in convincing even the most senior of doctors that they are in agony and have something very seriously wrong with them. I had come across several such patients during my earlier career, both in Blackburn and Blackpool. There was one young man, in particular, who was habitually admitted for abdominal pain and usually found to have swallowed an infinite variety of foreign objects, quite unbelievably including knives, forks and spoons. The number of times he had undergone surgery to have these items removed was quite mind-boggling and yet when he was recovering and being cared for in hospital he was happy as a sand boy.

In Margaret's case, she was an accomplished actress and could easily have won an award for her many outstanding performances. It would have been a particularly brave or reckless doctor, indeed, who ignored the completely imaginary but extremely convincing symptoms with which she presented herself at Casualty. Her medical records were overwhelmingly comprehensive and extensive, yet following all the admissions, tests and examinations over the years, nothing concrete had ever been found. Each time she came in, I was strongly reminded of the story of the child who cried wolf because one day there really would be something genuinely, medically, wrong with Margaret. In that situation, she was much more likely to be ignored, possibly with potential fatal consequences, and the poor unwitting medic attending her would no doubt be struck off or sued for negligence.

The cost to the NHS every year for just one patient such as Margaret is astronomical, and yet sadly there is no real treatment that can be offered to any of them, and many find themselves on a permanent merry-go-round of hospital admissions and doctors' appointments throughout their unhappy lives. Despite feeling truly sorry for these unfortunate individuals, they could be an absolute nightmare when staff and resources were hard pressed.

Yet here she was again, looking every inch the drama queen. As always, regardless of our suspicions, we would be obliged to err on the side of caution and check her out thoroughly, in case she was not messing us about. Thankfully there are many ways to check if a patient is genuinely unconscious. An unconscious patient will not respond in any way to external stimuli, regardless of the discomfort. One such test is to apply firm pressure over sensitive areas of the body (particularly over the pressure points), for example pressing hard over the breastbone or even on the centre line of the eyebrow or throat. Flicking a patient's eyelashes will get no response if they are unconscious, whereas they will flinch with surprise if not. There are numerous alternatives (not all in the textbooks!), but these are the ones most commonly used.

As we couldn't get near enough to carry out any such checks, Eileen started to shake Margaret's feet and shout out her name. I waited patiently for a few seconds, watching out for the slightest indication that she was aware of my presence looking down on her. She kept absolutely still; there was not even a flicker. This woman was good. Not to be beaten, I grabbed a handful of paper towels and soaked them under the cold water tap. I slowly squeezed the wet towels over her face, dripping big drops across her tightly shut eyes and forehead. The unexpected shock of the cold water induced an involuntary movement, then very slowly, but still without looking up to see where the water was coming from, she altered the position of her head ever so slightly to allow the water to drain away. Observing her do this I felt quite vindicated, as I now knew for certain that this was yet one more of her spurious attempts to gain admittance to hospital. Making absolutely sure that this result was not a fluke, I squeezed out one or two more drops, this time around her mouth, and almost immediately Margaret's lips parted a little and the tip of her tongue flicked out to lick the water away.

That was it; as far as I was concerned, she had confirmed our suspicions. I jumped down from the washbasin and knocked hard on the cubicle door, shouting her name and demanding she come out immediately. There was neither sound nor sign of movement. After advising her in no uncertain terms that we had observed her reactions and knew she was faking, we told her that we had genuine patients to see; then pretended to leave. We opened and closed the outer door and stood quietly to one side, waiting to see if she emerged from the cubicle. Seconds later, the black shoes disappeared from sight back under the door and we could hear her huffing and puffing and swearing under her breath as she tried to get up off the floor (which wasn't easy in such a confined space). She tentatively opened the door a fraction to peep out, then recoiled in surprise when she saw us both standing there looking straight at her. A look of resignation spread over her face as she realised that the game was well and truly up, though with one final flourish she still tried to maintain that she had come over 'all dizzy' and blacked out, insisting that she still needed to see a doctor.

'If that's the case, Margaret,' I urged, 'you are welcome to go to reception and book yourself in, but you will have to wait your turn like everyone else.'

Deciding to retreat on this occasion and try again another day, she brushed herself down, straightened her hair in the mirror and shuffled out through the exit doors into the freezing cold night, muttering to herself how sorry we would be when she was found frozen to death in a ditch somewhere. Despite our frustration, the whole situation was so dreadfully sad that we didn't really know how to react or to feel. She was a total nuisance, but she was also a fellow human being in need of a little love and affection. We waved our farewells, told her to take care and wished her a Happy New Year when it came around. She never even glanced back, simply made her way down the approach road like a woman on a mission, probably planning her next illness.

Sadly, Margaret's situation was far from uncommon and in years gone by these patients would have quite likely found themselves being forcibly admitted to a psychiatric institution rather than being ushered back into the community. Hospitals around the country would occasionally send out fax messages to warn neighbouring health authorities about such Walter Mitty characters doing the rounds. Some would get themselves admitted and demand specific named drugs for pain relief. Often these were simply desperate people who had become addicted to prescription medicines, originally given to them by their GPs for chronic pain relief. As underlying medical conditions gradually improve and less pain relief is needed, it requires very careful handling to help wean patients off their medication, thus avoiding acute withdrawal symptoms (which for some can be as debilitating as their original illness). For others it is simply a cry for attention, a ruse in order to be noticed and loved.

Drug addicts were the third category of patients most likely to appear out of the blue purporting to have dubious ailments and demanding specific medications to make them better; especially DF118, Valium and temazepam, all of which have a high street value. They can get extremely vociferous, standing their ground, arguing vehemently (even with the doctors) and using hastily learnt medical jargon in order to sound *au fait* with their ostensible medical conditions. A great deal of time is wasted ringing GPs or other hospitals to check out their stories, verify their identities and confirm what treatments they are legally receiving. It was again both sad and infuriating to see and hear these individuals who went to such drastic and desperate lengths to get their fix.

Once Margaret was well on her way and not likely to come back that night, Eileen and I were able to get back to the long-suffering patients we had been obliged to forsake due to this little charade. We apologised for having kept them waiting and most of them were very understanding. Mind you, that was because they were blissfully unaware of the actual circumstances for the delay; they were convinced that Eileen and I had been saving someone's life. If only they knew, they would probably have lynched poor Margaret in the waiting room.

Chapter 6

8.20pm

Eileen and I arrived back in the minor injuries area to find Sister Barnett wondering where we had got to. She shook her head in despair when we told her that Margaret had been up to her old tricks again. Apparently she had been in twice that week already, each time with yet another fascinating story and a different assortment of ailments, and we could only hope that she wouldn't turn up again anytime soon.

Sister had dealt with Moses as a priority and put some stitches in the cut on his head, mainly in order for the accompanying officers to get back on duty rather than them having to sit around waiting for him to be treated but also to avoid any further disruption. Before being allowed to leave the department he was examined by the doctor, who wanted to make sure that he wasn't concussed, then after he had been declared fit to be discharged the self-professed leader of the

Israelites was escorted to the waiting police van to be taken into custody, now singing and waving merrily as he was dragged away.

By this time, the doctors looked tired out, having been on duty since early morning. It was now some nine and a half hours later and they had been working virtually non-stop without a proper meal break, but were no doubt hoping to get their hands on some of the party food which the night staff were expected to be bringing in. Unlike the nurses who were about to go off duty, there were still another 90 long minutes of their shift to get through and all they desperately wanted to do now was go home, have a hot meal and slump in front of the box for a couple of hours. It was extremely doubtful that any of them would be going out partying; some had families to consider and, in any case, they were much too exhausted. Dr Davies groaned when we told him that two new patients had just arrived on the minor injuries side and were now awaiting his attendance.

It was now 8.25pm and almost time for the night staff to make an appearance. I had only been on duty two and a half hours, yet it felt like I'd been working all day. However, there was a rejuvenating buzz in the air as the new shift arrived for duty in good spirits, all geared up and determined not to be miserable just because they had to see in the new year at work.

Sister Clipboard suddenly appeared out of nowhere, all smiling and friendly, telling the night staff how busy it had been and how she couldn't wait to get her feet up. I was gobsmacked and my face must have said it all. No one said a word, but the silent looks between the rest of the day staff spoke volumes, and one or two of the night staff grinned knowingly as they locked their bags away and prepared for the night ahead.

Before the day staff could disappear a loud, high-pitched scream was heard coming from the ambulance bay. For a moment we all looked at each other, nobody moving, wondering who on earth could be making such a din, then as the manic cries increased in volume, I volunteered to go and investigate while the night staff gathered in the treatment area in preparation for the formal handover between the two shifts.

Two ambulance men were struggling manfully in an effort to prevent an elderly lady from falling off a stretcher, although she was fighting and screaming like a mad woman, all I could make out was a blur of arms and legs, punching and kicking out at the bemused men as they tried to pacify this veritable tigress. Everything became crystal clear as soon as I saw who she was; Emily was another one of our regulars. She was an insulin-dependent diabetic who had an unfortunate tendency to neglect to manage her condition.

Insulin is a hormone which is produced naturally in the body by the pancreas to help the body use the glucose in food as energy. An insulin-dependent diabetic's pancreas produces little or no natural insulin so they have to inject themselves on a daily basis. If insufficient food is consumed after injecting, there is a danger that the blood sugar levels (i.e. glucose levels) can become too low, which causes hypoglycaemia. If the condition isn't treated promptly the patient falls into a coma.

As Emily was elderly and sometimes neglected to eat after taking her insulin, she had been known to become hypoglycaemic before. In fact she would all too regularly be brought into Casualty after having been found in a highly confused and sometimes aggressive state.

If a person does become hypoglycaemic, one way of treating it is to consume carbohydrates in some form or other (such as a glucose lozenge, a digestive biscuit, a slice of bread or even a small chocolate bar) until the blood glucose level rises. This is how a diabetic would normally cure themselves, but Emily's condition had already pro-gressed too far. As the hypoglycaemia progresses, sufferers react in many different ways; they become increasingly fatigued, agitated and confused, occasionally becoming violent and irrational, too. Emily no longer had the ability to make rational decisions and she refused all our offers of the usual carbohydrates so we knew she might be in real danger.

A person doesn't necessarily have to be diabetic to become hypoglycaemic. Athletes who train hard and use up all their energy need to top up with carbohydrates constantly, which is why professional tennis players and many other sportsmen are often seen munching bananas or drinking energy drinks during their matches/games in order to prevent themselves becoming debilitated. Coincidentally, doctors running around on long shifts and missing meals are also prime candidates.

Virtually everyone at some time or other has days when they feel unwell and don't want to eat or can't be bothered to cook a meal. Unfortunately, a diabetic can't afford to do this. Despite having a very supportive family and fantastic neighbours, who often provided meals for her or did her shopping, Emily was forever turning up in Casualty with these symptoms. The problem was that if she didn't like the food she was given she threw it away, or some days she simply didn't feel like eating anything at all. After the ambulance crew had placed Emily in one of the examination rooms, I asked them if they would stay with her while I went for a glucometer (an instrument to check her blood sugar levels) and a pre-packed intravenous glucose solution (which needed to be administered immediately if her levels were too low).

A quick hello to Emily was rewarded with a vociferous, 'Bugger off,' that brought a few smiles. One ambulance man held her arm as steady as he could while I quickly checked her blood sugar. As expected, it was very low. I went to find Dr Burn, who was more than a little amused to see all three of us struggling to keep one little old lady subdued. When he saw just how low her levels were, though, he swiftly injected her directly into the vein with the glucose solution.

I was absolutely fascinated the first time I watched a diabetic patient being given intravenous glucose, which corrects the imbalance very rapidly. The patient was virtually in a coma and not responsive, yet within seconds of receiving the injection (in fact, while the doctor still had the needle in her arm) the lady came around and started chatting to us, wondering what on earth she was doing in hospital.

A similar transformation happened with Emily and in next to no time she had quietened down and started to look around, trying to get her bearings. She gave a huge grin when she saw three burly men and me looking down at her, hanging on to an arm or a leg each in case she went berserk again. As if butter wouldn't melt, she sheepishly inquired, 'Have I been a naughty girl again?'

We all had a good laugh as the two ambulance men limped exaggeratedly around the room, pretending to be permanently lamed from her assaults. She apologised unreservedly and solemnly promised that it wouldn't happen again, but I don't believe any of us were totally convinced. She was kept in the observation unit for a while until the casualty doctors were completely satisfied that she was fit to go home. Her daughter arrived soon afterwards, having been alerted to Emily's plight by a neighbour. She sat with Emily, gave her a good telling off (no doubt feeling a little embarrassed at having to collect her mother from Casualty yet again) and assured us she would keep a much closer eye on her in the future. Promises were made that she would never darken our doorstep again, but we weren't going to hold our breath.

As she was being wheeled outside to be taken home, Emily gave us all a great big smile and said, 'See you soon.'

What a gem – it was difficult to be angry with a lonely old lady who inadvertently risked her own life by failing to maintain a strictly correct diet twenty-four hours a day, seven days a week.

Astounding as the rapid recovery following an injection of glucose to remedy a hypoglycaemic episode may seem, this doesn't hold a candle to a treatment I have witnessed given to seriously ill babies. After qualifying as an SRN in 1971, one of my first jobs was working at Park Lee Hospital in Blackburn on the Isolation Unit for infectious diseases. A baby boy, about eight weeks old, was admitted via Casualty suffering from severe dehydration after several hours of non-stop diarrhoea and vomiting. The child was grey, limp and near to death. Having already witnessed a couple of cot deaths in Casualty, I was extremely dubious about his chances of survival. The paediatrician came hurrying in and, taking one look at this poor child, immediately requested that I draw up an injection of hydrocortisone as quickly as possible. After some initial difficulty in finding a vein, he managed to insert a very fine Venflon into the child's scalp. With a smug look on his face he whispered, 'Just watch this.'

Literally within seconds the baby started to breathe properly and turn pink, screaming his little lungs out, legs rigid and fists clenched in temper. After a few tears (and not just from me), our patient was put on a drip. Two or three days later, when he had fully recovered, he was returned home perfectly fit and well.

Since that time I have seen this apparently miraculous recovery on a number of occasions. In essence, the cortisone acts almost immediately by stimulating the adrenal glands, thus increasing the child's low blood pressure and reducing any inflammation, which rapidly allows the child's heart and lungs to perform normally. It is always a supremely satisfying reaction to witness.

Working nights on Casualty is very different from working the day shift. Of course, there are still patients with the same old, routine, basic injuries and ailments, but at night in all Casualty departments there are far more alcohol- and drug-fuelled incidents and accidents that can make the units buzz with noise and outright aggression. When I first started work at Wythenshawe, it struck me how young, friendly and feisty the nurses on nights were compared to their generally much quieter, middle-aged counterparts on the day shifts. Nothing ever seemed to disrupt the professional demeanour of these (mainly) young female staff who appeared able to cope fearlessly in aggressive confrontational situations or when dealing with uncooperative individuals hell-bent on starting trouble. More often than not, it was usually the most diminutive nurses who (against all odds) remained polite and confident when faced with a huge, drunken bruiser shouting and swearing in their faces after being asked to behave.

I always remember the occasion when a young, rather well-spoken female house officer from the medical ward came into the department to examine a man who had taken an overdose. The patient she had been called to see was so drunk he was practically paralytic and was using language no longer tolerated on the football terraces. This inexperienced doctor, who was in her first post after qualifying, simply hadn't a clue how to deal with him and found herself blushing furiously when he started making totally outrageous and vile suggestions and sexual innuendoes. One of the nurses, who just happened to be passing the overdose room, overheard the conversation and immediately went to her assistance. Quite amazingly, while remaining polite at all times and never once raising her voice, within minutes she had him eating out of her hand.

The drunk apologised to the doctor, who had stood aside in awe while she watched this slip of a girl gain the upper hand over the lout, and he remained on his best behaviour while she completed her examination. Before leaving the department this doctor made a beeline to thank the nurse for her support and asked her what the secret was. She just shrugged her shoulders and laughingly replied that it would get easier with practice. As a rule, the calmer the staff, the better behaved the patient seemed to be.

Sister Jeanne Mansfield was in charge of the night shift tonight and was due to take over from Sister Barnett and Sister Clipboard. From the looks of her, she was ready for anything. Organised and efficient, she was highly experienced and also well respected by her colleagues and staff. Never one to hide away from work and always leading the line, she was one of the three senior sisters in charge who covered the seven night shifts each week between them. Although very different in character, without exception Jeanne, Audrey and Joan were always ready and willing to roll up their sleeves and work hard alongside the rest of us. Jeanne was one of the most easygoing sisters in the department; she never, ever raised her voice in anger, treated everyone fairly and rarely lost her temper, not even with the multitude of swearing, fighting-mad drunks who regularly crossed her path. And, believe me, that took some doing.

Also working alongside me and Jeanne for the night shift were three other staff nurses, Wendy, Kath and Cynthia, and two enrolled nurses, Chris(tine) and Theresa. (The doctors and receptionist worked slightly different hours to the nursing staff and were due to change over at 10pm.) Whenever Wendy was on duty there always seemed to be a great deal of laughter coming from whichever section of the department she happened to be working. Having spent several years working the night shift in Casualty, it had become like a home from home for her and, like many of the other nurses, she was able to deal amazingly well with anything and everything that came through the doors. Her bubbly personality, laid-back approach and natural ability to put people at their ease quickly helped patients to feel less apprehensive about being brought into hospital, and to make them relax she would always make light of any situation if she could. During the years I worked with her, I also found her to have a photographic memory. If she recognised a patient from a previous visit, without the aid of any medical records she could invariably remember their name, what they had been to Casualty for, what tests they had undergone and what treatment they received. Sometimes patients who suffered a whole variety of chronic medical problems that necessitated taking numerous different daily medications (which many of them often carried around in their pockets like trophies) would delight in giving the doctor a blow by blow account of every single hospital and GP visit they had ever attended, together with a long list of every operation and ailment they had suffered since drawing their first breath. The doctors occasionally glazed over and almost lost the plot when trying to document all this information (especially if the patient wasn't from the area and the doctor had no access to any of their medical records) but Wendy could usually repeat virtually word for word everything the patient had said, so if the doctor ever missed something she was invariably able to come to the rescue. She confided to me on several occasions that, had she not become a nurse, she would have liked to complete a law degree and perhaps specialise in healthcare litigation. I had no doubt that she would have excelled in whatever her chosen occupation may have been. In general, all the nurses coming on duty were bubbly characters who I greatly enjoyed working with.

Finally, there was an older lady on duty called Anita, who, to my knowledge, never really had a proper job title as such. She was due to retire before too long, after having worked for many years on nights in the staff canteen (until the hot food service she provided had been withdrawn in preference to the cheaper alternative of pre-prepared microwave meals). Because Anita was so close to retirement she was kept on and became one of two 'helpers' whose vague job description was to assist the nurses in any non-medical way possible. She cleared and changed the sheets on empty trolleys when they became vacant, restocked the medical supplies, gave out bedpans and made hot drinks for patients and their relatives, but her most outstanding feature was her quiet, gentle nature. Anita was a real sweetheart and everyone loved her to bits, especially the older patients who were sometimes brought in alone and needed someone to support them. There was always a ready smile on her face and she was never heard to complain. Working with the first-class casualty team at Wythenshawe was my privilege but, for some reason, I always felt more at home with this particular group on nights than any other.

The night staff all seemed up for the challenge ahead, although there were only two stretcher cases and a couple of minor injuries still waiting to be dealt with; everything else was tidy and shelves were well stocked. They couldn't believe how quiet it was although we all had grave doubts it would last too much longer. It wasn't unusual for the night shift to find themselves thrust into the middle of a noisy, untidy battlefield, so tonight certainly made a welcome change. That was one of the problems that arose from working on both the day and night shifts; sometimes, when staff had been too busy to replenish stocks or clean the trolleys and stretchers between shifts, I would be requested to have a quiet word with the others. At first I felt like piggy in the middle, but I quickly resolved to keep my own counsel; if there was a problem then, as far as I was concerned, it was up to the sister in charge of that particular shift to deal with it themselves and not me.

The handover between the shifts normally takes about ten or fifteen minutes, but this is, of course, dependent on how many patients there are at the time. The sister or senior staff nurse on day duty passes on to every member of the night shift all relevant information about any patients still in the department (or in the process of being x-rayed and expected to return to the unit). The day staff were already getting ready to go home and I was looking forward to the freedom of being able to work more flexibly so, while the handover (and the general girly gossip) was still being made, I decided to have a quick look into room number one on the stretcher side to check on the patient in there.

A young woman in her mid-twenties was being investigated for possible appendicitis. She'd already had several blood specimens taken about half an hour earlier, which were currently being processed in the laboratory, and she was now waiting to go to X-ray. When I popped my head around the door to reassure her that it wouldn't be too long before she was sorted out, the poor girl looked lost and was having a quiet weep, so I inquired whether anyone had come with her and if she wanted me to bring them in to keep her company. She perked up a little and asked if I wouldn't mind going to get her husband to come and sit with her. I went out into the waiting area, despite not really knowing who I was looking for, but there was not a soul in sight and all was uncannily quiet. Thinking that he might have gone outside for a smoke or to the toilet, I waited in reception for a few minutes before checking again. There was no one outside and the only sign of life was an elderly gentleman hunched over in the corner of the waiting room asleep. I went back to the young woman and told her that I couldn't find him anywhere.

Without thinking I went on to say, 'There is only one little old man in the waiting room and he is fast asleep.'

'That's him,' she said, bristling with indignation.

'It can't be,' I said, instantly dismissing the possibility and continuing to excavate a huge crater for myself. 'No, really, it can't be him. The man I'm talking about is old enough to be your grandfather.'

'That IS him,' she insisted. 'He IS my husband. Please can you bring him in?'

I was just about to insist for a third time before finally thinking better of it and, thankfully, keeping my mouth firmly shut. I apologised sincerely for my gaffe and rushed out to get him. I didn't know whether to laugh or not, but how was I to know that these two ill-matched people were married? I still found it difficult to believe that this could be the correct person, but nevertheless I gently shook him awake and asked if he wanted to come and sit with his wife. It took him a minute or so before he was sufficiently awake to drag himself to his feet and shuffle along behind me. The patient was clearly used to others making such a mistake and simply frowned at my embarrassment as I showed the now out-of-breath old chap into her room.

Shortly afterwards the young woman was taken around to X-ray where she had several abdominal films taken, before being returned to her room to wait for the results. Having already made one outsize blunder, I interrupted the hand-over and pre-warned the rest of the staff to be careful what they said. Obviously grateful for the information, they all had a good laugh at my expense.

All her x-rays and blood results turned out to be normal,

in the end, so she was given a few antispasmodics for the pain and advised to see her own GP for advice on healthy eating (her eventual diagnosis being constipation!). One or two of the nurses who saw this gentleman escorting his child bride out, said they thought he actually looked old enough to be her great-grandfather. Such is life, I suppose, but it reminded me once again to engage my brain before letting my mouth take control.

Chapter 7

8.40pm

The day nurses had now come to the end of the handover and were standing around discussing their plans for the evening ahead, while waiting for Sister Barnett to give them the go-ahead to leave. Valerie's last stretcher patient was all but ready to be moved up to the ward and so she filled me in. Edith, an elderly lady with chest pain, had been checked out thoroughly by the doctor from the medical ward prior to admitting her. Although she was not showing any obvious changes on her heart tracing at that time (which would have suggested that she had suffered a coronary), the symptoms were classic. She had been experiencing a crushing pain in her chest radiating down her left arm for most of the day; but it was only when her daughter came to visit that evening and observed just how poorly she looked that an ambulance was called. There was definitely something brewing (very similar to the gentleman earlier on, who had discharged himself) and the doctor had felt it advisable to keep her in for observation. I called for a porter and offered to accompany her to the medical ward, expecting to be away from the department no more than a few minutes.

We chatted about her large family and life in general as we made our way along the lengthy corridors. Edith was an experienced old hand as a patient and had been admitted to hospital on several occasions for a whole variety of problems, including previous chest and heart complaints, and appeared to be quite accepting of her present predicament. She was still happily making small talk as we entered the lift to take her up to Ward F7 on the second floor, a general medical ward situated at the furthest point of another very long corridor.

Just before the lift arrived at its destination, I realised that my patient, who had been talking incessantly since leaving Casualty, had gone ominously quiet. I was behind the raised back rest of the stretcher and pinned against the wall, but from my position in the lift, I spoke to Edith to advise her that we were almost there. I received no reply, so I edged my way around the side of the trolley to take a quick peep to see if she was OK. To my dismay, she was slumped against the pillows with her head to one side, her mouth dangling open and drooling saliva. Her skin was cold and clammy with a definite blue tinge (meaning that she was not getting enough oxygen); her eyes were wide open but unseeing. I shouted Edith's name and shook her shoulders vigorously, but there was still no reaction. Feeling for a pulse and checking her respirations, I swiftly realised that she was not breathing and was in cardiac arrest. I was dumbfounded. She had given no indication whatsoever that she was in any sort of discomfort, so whatever happened must have been pretty rapid. The porter, who up to this point had been totally oblivious to our conversation, looked scared to death and, to be honest, I wasn't exactly thrilled to be stuck in a claustrophobically small restricted space with a patient in dire need of cardio pulmonary resuscitation (CPR) either. To make matters much worse, apart from an oxygen cylinder and mask, we had no specialist equipment with us to carry out anything other than manual resuscitation. Here we were in a lift, hundreds of yards away from Casualty and still at the opposite end of a very long corridor from the ward where we were expected. As I rapidly lay the patient flat on her back, cleared her airway and commenced CPR, the lift arrived at the second floor. The doors seemed to take forever to open, but once we were out on the corridor I shouted to the porter to run us into the first available ward we came to (which, unfortunately for the staff there, happened to be the gynaecology ward) and head for their treatment room. Running while trying to simultaneously push a heavy trolley and do CPR is not to be recommended; by the time we reached Ward F5, I was already shattered and struggling to breathe myself. The nurses on the ward were in the middle of giving out the night-time drinks to the patients and weren't expecting such dramas. They looked quite shell-shocked as the stretcher burst through the ward doors with me virtually riding on top, kneeling precariously next to the patient, frantically pounding away on Edith's chest giving cardiac massage and providing mouth to mouth resuscitation, and shouting for someone to dial 333 to summon the crash team.

Every hospital nowadays has its own crash team, which usually comprises a number of junior and senior doctors (but always includes an anaesthetist), who are on call to attend anywhere in the hospital whenever there is a cardiac arrest. Every ward and department has its own stock of resuscitation equipment and emergency drugs available for such eventualities and, in the case of a cardiac arrest, all staff know there is a specific pre-arranged emergency telephone number to be used by everyone throughout the hospital. This number immediately alerts the switchboard, who in turn bleeps all members of the on-call team and directs them to the correct area. A group of doctors running like the clappers, white coats flapping behind them, hardly able to breathe themselves with the effort, adrenaline spiking in anticipation of being confronted by a patient about to meet their maker at any second, are a fairly regular sight in most hospitals. As a staff nurse at Blackburn Royal Infirmary years earlier, the cardiac crash team came bursting through the ward doors after running virtually the full length of the hospital, but then ended up working on two heart attack victims simultaneously when one of the doctors in the crash team dropped down dead and couldn't be resuscitated. He was thirty-eight years old.

The nurses' faces fleetingly registered panic and I am sure one or two must have been having palpitations as their ordered routine was so rudely interrupted. At first everything seemed to be moving in slow motion, but once they realised what was happening they quickly got themselves organised. While we rushed the stretcher into the treatment room, one staff nurse ran to the nearest telephone and called for the crash team while another pulled out their resuscitation trolley and attached Edith to a heart monitor. Someone else inserted an oral airway into her mouth (a black, J-shaped plastic tube designed to keep the mouth and throat clear thus allowing the patient to breathe easier and prevent her swallowing her tongue) and placed an Ambu bag (handheld ventilator) over her nose and mouth to give her regulated oxygen. And, finally, another nurse prepared a syringe of adrenaline ready to be handed to the crash team as soon as they arrived. I was still carrying out cardiac massage as the crash team ran on to the ward less than two minutes later. They virtually fell through the doors of the treatment room, all of them out of breath and perspiring from their exertions, and were momentarily puzzled to see me pumping away on this elderly woman's chest on top of a casualty stretcher. My cap had gone walkabout somewhere along the main corridor and I could scarcely catch my breath with the effort of trying to get this lady's heart restarted.

'What are you doing here, Woodcock?' said one bright spark (having seen me only a short time earlier down in Casualty), as he dragged me off the trolley so he could take over.

'I was bored in Casualty, so I thought I would liven F5 up,' I said, gasping for breath and trying to speak at the same time.

Hands on hips, one of the staff nurses pulled a face to express mock displeasure that I had brought such total chaos to their normally peaceful existence. At this juncture I also thought it prudent to mention to the doctors that I thought Edith may require a chest x-ray at some point because, during the course of my efforts at cardiac massage, I was pretty sure that I had broken one or two of the patient's ribs. When I first pressed down hard over her sternum I definitely felt something give way with a sickening crunch. The crash team looked as if they were about to start making some derogatory comments so, since they now seemed to have assumed complete control, I quickly made an exit to advise Ward F7 what was happening. It was only polite to alert the ward sister, seeing as Edith was technically their patient. I was glad in retrospect that none of Edith's relatives had been with us, as they would normally have accompanied us on our journey up to the ward to keep her company. It is always particularly distressing when something like this happens in front of loved ones. Thankfully, they had decided to find their own way up to the ward and had gone ahead of us some ten minutes earlier and were by now probably wondering if we had got lost.

I hurried into Sister's office and explained what had happened in the lift. She listened to me intently then, without mentioning anything to Edith's relatives who were all sat outside waiting for her, she advised her senior staff nurse what had happened and instructed her to move one or two beds around so that Edith could be placed nearer to the nurses' station where they could keep a close eye on her. She requested a cardiac monitor and resuscitation equipment be made ready just in case and, while these were being organised, Sister came back to F5 with me to see if anything more could be done and to offer her assistance.

Although all nurses are trained to do CPR, the staff on medical wards/casualty were far more used to dealing with cardiac arrests (because of the type of patients they cared for) than the nurses on the gynaecology ward, who would rarely see even one such case a year. Having said that, once the girls on F5 realised what was happening, their training kicked in and they did a great job. By the time we arrived from F7 there was very little for Sister to do, other than provide a reassuring presence.

The very first time I had to carry out cardiac massage on an actual patient was on the female medical ward when I was a young student. One of the ladies used her buzzer to summon me to say that the patient in the next bed had fallen over to one side and appeared to be unwell. Trying not to panic too much I asked her to press her buzzer three times in quick succession, as this was the recognised distress call which would alert the other members of staff to an emergency situation. After having checked in vain for a pulse, I pulled the curtains around the bed and began CPR. Help arrived almost immediately in the form of Sister and two student nurses.

The beds in use at that time were very old-fashioned and hopeless if you were trying to do cardiac massage (they simply weren't firm enough), so while I attempted to start massage anyway, one nurse ran to fetch the resuscitation trolley that contained all the necessary equipment and drugs. The other nurse rushed to call the doctor and on the way back collected a wooden board that was kept in the treatment room specifically to place underneath the patient but on top of the mattress, to provide a much firmer working surface. With the board in place, I clambered back on to the bed and started pumping up and down on her chest as we had been shown in training school. Sister ensured the patient's airway was clear and administered oxygen while simultaneously giving mouth to mouth resuscitation. The doctor arrived soon afterwards and gave the patient the necessary cocktail of drugs while I continued massaging her heart. Thankfully, after working on her for the longest few minutes of my life, she began to respond. No amount of practice on a dummy can ever make up for the real thing, though, which is exhausting, exhilarating and sheer physical hard work. The lady survived and made a full recovery but for days afterwards I could hardly raise my arms because my biceps virtually seized up due to the unusual strain on muscles that you do not usually use, unless you are in the gym doing a workout.

Over the years in Casualty, use of cardiac massage on collapsed patients becomes an everyday occurrence but it is never easy and doing it properly for more than about ten minutes at a time is almost impossible. If the patient had a video recording of some nurse or doctor kneeling on top of the trolley, beating the hell out of their chest in an attempt to get their heart started, they would be shocked. But then again, they would have to be alive to appreciate it. So far this shift, my strong arm techniques had been called upon twice (although the night was still young) and my arms already felt like lead weights. If they were uncomfortable now, heaven only knows what they would feel like tomorrow morning!

The doctors worked hard on Edith, giving her a number of drugs, including intra-venous adrenaline, and continued with CPR until she eventually began to show signs of recovery. A bleep on the cardiac monitor heralded a regular strong heartbeat and her blood pressure soon reached acceptable levels. Within minutes she opened her eyes and tried to drag her oxygen mask off, until gentle persuasion from several staff convinced her to leave it in place. She then looked around the room and started chatting away again as if nothing had happened. Once the doctors felt that she was stable enough to be moved, Sister introduced herself and held her hand while she was quickly pushed along to F7. Once she was tucked up in bed, I removed the stretcher, thanked everyone for their assistance and set off pushing it along the corridor back to Casualty by myself (retrieving my starched cap along the way, which was still on the floor outside the lift). The porter had abandoned me at some point, but for the life of me I couldn't remember seeing him go. In any event that was probably the most sensible thing for him to have done, as he couldn't help any further on F5 but could obviously now be getting on with other jobs in the meantime. Mind you, after seeing the shock on his face in the lift, I think he was glad to get away, and who could blame him?

Later that night, while returning from escorting another patient to the ward, I came across one of the doctors from the crash team wandering along the main corridor, looking exhausted after having dealt with his fourth cardiac arrest of the evening. He told me that soon after I left F7, Edith had begun to complain about a sharp pain in her chest, especially when she breathed in. A chest x-ray confirmed, as I suspected, that she did indeed have a couple of fractured ribs, but apart from that she was doing fine. He patted me on the back and said that I had done a great job, but warned me with a wry smile that he didn't want to see me again that night! Many doctors argue that unless you break a rib during cardiac massage you aren't doing it properly; although I am not sure everyone would agree with that philosophy. I was chuffed to hear that Edith was going to be OK, despite feeling a modicum of regret at having caused her some additional discomfort. I consoled myself that, when the chips were down, she no doubt preferred being in pain to being dead.

I was well and truly shattered after running up and down several long corridors like a mad woman. When I eventually returned to Casualty the staff had already been brought up to speed by the elusive porter and, as expected, a few unflattering opinions were expressed regarding my ability to spread death and destruction wherever I went. It seemed like I had been away from the department for hours, when it was in fact little more than thirty minutes, but I felt and looked like I had been dragged through a hedge backwards. My hair was all over the place and I hadn't yet replaced my cap, which was now also looking much the worse for wear.

The day staff were long gone (and no doubt some would already be getting ready to enjoy the evening festivities, at least the ones with any energy left to do so) and the department was again ticking over nicely. There still seemed to be a steady stream of patients injured after falling on the icy pavements and an increasing number of early drunken revellers, as well as several ambulance cases who were being attended by doctors Burn and Pickering. I apologised to Jeanne for being away so long, but she assured me that I hadn't missed anything interesting, and she suggested I get myself tidied up and go for a quick cuppa, as the day staff had told her I hadn't yet had a chance to take my break. I didn't refuse; there was very little I could be doing in any case because all the patients were already being dealt with, so I took advantage of the offer while I could.

Night casualty staff were normally expected to take their break in the staff room rather than the hospital canteen, simply because we needed to be near the department and immediately available if there was a sudden influx of emergency cases. Because the night staff had only just come on duty, I was on my lonesome this time and just settled for a quick cup of tea before going back. From the staff room windows it was possible to see any ambulance coming down the approach road and also the pedestrian entrance where people were dropped off or made their own way in. Sometimes we would play a juvenile game to amuse ourselves before we went back to work, which involved trying to guess what was wrong with someone from the way they were walking. Broken legs and haemorrhoids were the easy favourites. Our staff room was quite a popular venue in those days, not only for the doctors, nurses and receptionists but also half of Greater Manchester Police. Most Casualty departments have a close working relationship with their local police officers and Wythenshawe was no exception. We relied on their support a great deal because there was little internal security within the hospital in those days and, besides which, they were always in and out with prisoners who occasionally needed medical attention; although these were more often than not just drunk and incapable, we were still obliged to check them all out. Many of the local officers used our staff room as a regular stop during their long night shifts and their presence deterred much petty vandalism, plus they would also make the odd drink for the staff if we were busy. It wasn't really skiving, it was building a good working relationship and even the senior officers would sometimes pop in to check up on us and see that all was well.

One night a police dog-handler was sitting with us having a coffee when one of the girls asked where his dog was. Despite animals being banned from the hospital, he was persuaded to bring the dog into the outer office for a biscuit. This beautiful German Shepherd, the size of a small Shetland pony, was soon demolishing ginger nuts and lying on his back having his belly tickled by half the staff. Someone remarked that the dog wasn't very scary and didn't look like it would frighten anybody. The officer confided that each handler had a trigger word that was used to get the dog to show aggression, and, holding firmly onto its lead he said, 'Keep away and don't try to touch him.'

He whispered something in the animal's ear and it

immediately turned the dog into a snarling bundle of teeth and fur that no one in their right mind would think of approaching. Another whispered command and the dog was once again all sweetness and light.

Fascinated, a couple of the nurses pressed the officer to tell them what the trigger word was. He refused to share this information and maintained his silence on the subject for several minutes, but when they wouldn't let the matter drop he eventually relented. The word used was quite politically incorrect, but after having to listen to the vile language commonly used by a significant minority of our patients, none of the staff present could possibly have been in the least bit shocked by it. Sadly, however, someone reported the matter to the officer's superiors and he was moved back to normal duties and no longer allowed to work with his dog. I felt really sad that someone could be so underhand, even though he probably shouldn't have allowed himself to be persuaded to bring the dog into the hospital in the first place, nor should he have divulged his trigger word to anyone. It was a hard lesson for all of us to learn and caused rather a strained atmosphere for a time between the nurses and some of the officers. We never did find out who had reported him.

Chapter 8

9.25pm

After the short break I threw myself back into the fray. Jeanne asked me to work with Theresa to clear a small backlog of minor injuries that had built up. We had just managed to clear most of them and Theresa was strapping up the sprained ankle of the last remaining patient, when three panic-stricken young men came rushing into the treatment area begging for our assistance. They had bypassed the receptionist, who was now hard on their heels and looking suitably put out at having been ignored. They had brought their friend to Casualty after finding him slumped on the floor of his flat, semi-conscious and reeking of alcohol with a suicide note lying beside him. The note said that he was sorry he had taken an overdose but he felt he couldn't face life any longer. He confessed to being afraid, scared of what he was going to have to face in the not-too-distant future, ashamed that he had brought disgrace and stigma on his family and on himself, and would prefer to be dead.

His friends had tried to make him vomit but without much success, so quite correctly they had decided to take matters into their own hands. They had forcibly bundled him into the back of their car, sobbing and incoherent as he was, and brought him to hospital as quickly as they could. Despite having got him this far, he was now refusing to get out of the car and was adamant that he wouldn't come into Casualty. He was absolutely inconsolable, begging his friends to leave him alone, pushing and kicking them away when they tried to drag him physically out of the vehicle.

Kath, who was working on the stretcher side and had overheard their conversation as she was tidying one of the rooms, immediately volunteered to come outside with me to see what could be done. Kath was a pretty, blonde girl several years younger than me who had worked in Casualty for a few years. Always very kind to the patients, from babes in arms to smelly unkempt tramps, she was a true patient advocate who would do anything to help them without a moment's hesitation. The three lads ran ahead of us to the car park as Kath and I grabbed a wheelchair and followed them out.

When we got to the car, the worried trio were again pleading with their friend to go into Casualty and at least talk to someone, but their pleas were being ignored and all we could hear was distraught, uncontrollable sobbing. Kath quietly urged the other lads away from the car to give me a chance to talk to him privately and to see if I could gain his confidence. She directed the three to reception, where Ann filled out a casualty card with the potential patient's general details, before taking them to one side to see if they could give her any further relevant information, such as what drugs he had actually taken, how long ago etc.

In the meantime, I climbed into the back seat of the car to have a talk to the young man. He sat there, covering his face with his hands, refusing even to look at me. After giving him a minute or so to compose himself, I introduced myself and asked if he would allow me to help him. At first, he continued to cry pitifully and shake his head, still declining even to make eye contact with me, choosing instead to stare vacantly at the floor in obvious despair. Eventually, with a bit of gentle persuasion, he opened up enough to tell me that his name was Luke and he was twenty-two years old.

Desperately trying to maintain a dialogue, I told him my Christian name (something we weren't really supposed to do) and asked if it was true that he had taken a number of pills and some alcohol. He simply nodded and once again began to sob, begging me to leave him alone and allow to him die. A few stragglers waiting for transport to take them home were hanging around outside and staring into the car to see what all the fuss was about, so when a number of drunken boisterous remarks started to be shouted at us through the open car door I begged Luke to go inside with me, where it was much warmer and where these spectators could not listen in to his private conversation.

My main concern, indeed the only thought that was uppermost in my mind as we spoke, was that the longer it took me to persuade him to be seen by a doctor, the more tablets were being absorbed into his system and the greater the potential risk to his chances of survival. I pleaded with him to open his eyes and look at me, assuring him that I was not there to judge but only wanted to help. Slowly but surely he began to open up, eventually telling me between big heartbroken sobs that he had been feeling exhausted and particularly unwell for several weeks. He had finally decided to consult his GP, who in turn had referred him to the Sexually Transmitted Disease Clinic at the hospital, where he had been subjected to a variety of blood tests and intimate swabs. At this point he broke down yet again, unwilling or unable even to discuss the outcome of these tests.

Without saying a word, I simply took hold of his hand and held it until he had regained his composure. Taking my time, I gently tried to persuade him to come with me into the department where he could perhaps tell the full story to a male doctor, so that he need only go through his story once without having to repeat it later. Reassuring him that no one would try to force or pressure him into accepting any treatments to which he didn't agree, I promised that I would stay with him at all times if he wished, in order to make sure that was the case. Although initially still refusing to leave the car, I was just about to suggest bringing the doctor out to him when, taking a really deep breath, he looked directly into my eyes and blurted out that his best friend had recently died from AIDS and that he had been informed by the clinic earlier today that he was HIV positive himself.

Now I clearly understood this pitiful young man's despair. There was relatively little known in the UK about HIV (Human Immunodeficiency Virus) at the time but it was considered by many doctors to be the precursor of a rather drawn-out and horrific death from full-blown AIDS (Acquired Immune Deficiency Syndrome), a disease where the HIV virus degrades and destroys the body's ability to fight off infection and disease.

The NHS was still quite uneducated in how to deal with such cases and many hospitals were ill-equipped to cope. Reported cases in the UK were still fairly few and far between, so clinicians were struggling to keep up with the current progress, care and treatments available and were really only just beginning to understand this debilitating disease. As with any newly identified illness there were so many conflicting theories and ideas that, sadly, until the doctors were absolutely sure what they were dealing with, sufferers faced being brought into hospital and kept in complete isolation, where everyone coming into contact with them had to wear surgical gowns, masks and gloves.

These unfortunate victims were commonly treated no better than lepers, even by some fearful hospital staff. It was a humiliating and frightening time both for them and their families, as well as for their friends and those who were caring for them.

As soon as Luke told me that he was HIV positive, I remember feeling extremely apprehensive and unsure what I should or shouldn't do next. I was, of course, aware that blood and bodily fluids could possibly transmit the virus, but that was the total extent of my knowledge. We had not been given any lectures or even written advice on how to cope with potential patients, yet here I was sitting next to an HIV positive man in a car, holding his hand and wiping away his tears. For one brief fleeting moment, my instinct was to drop his hand like a hot potato and jump out of the car, but clearly I couldn't do that. Of course, my first thoughts were for my family, who were always my overriding priority, but at this particular moment in time my job was to make Luke feel valued and cared for. He was desperately crying out for help and support, and, as a nurse, that was what my professional duty was all about. It isn't possible to pick and choose; you can't decide not to look after someone because you don't want to catch something from them. In all the years I have worked as a nurse, I can't recall a time when I ever considered refusing to deal with anyone because of my own personal safety (although I reserve the right to try and keep a bit of distance where fleas/body lice etc. are concerned!). The comprehensive basic practical training which I had received eighteen years ago had taught me about avoiding cross-infection and, providing I followed the usual strict guidelines, I should be OK. But there were no formal protocols in place for me to follow when it came to HIV, so in a way it was all in the lap of the gods.

Albeit reluctantly, Luke eventually agreed to come inside and I took him along to the overdose room while Kath went to find a doctor. Luke's friends had put her fully in the picture about his awful predicament and she had reassured them that Luke would be well looked after, before sending them all back into the waiting room.

I will never forget the kindness Dr Burn showed to Luke that night. Not the tallest person in the world, his dark hair and heart-throb good looks usually had the nurses at their most attentive when he needed assistance. He was also a friendly, pleasant person and an efficient physician. In my eyes he proved himself to be a thoroughly outstanding professional in the way he handled the situation with Luke. He introduced himself informally and shook his hand, reassuring him that he was there to help, but first and most importantly he needed to know what tablets he had taken and how long it had been since he had swallowed them. This was vital information because he had to make the crucial decision whether or not to wash out the patient's stomach. Luke said he'd swallowed an unknown number of paracetamol about an hour earlier, but had vomited only minutes after taking them, bringing most of the tablets back up almost immediately. Despite this, Dr Burn recommended to Luke that it was still safer to let us wash his stomach out, thus making sure it was completely empty and preventing any remaining harmful tablets being absorbed. (Paracetamol tablets are sold over the counter at any chemist and many people think they are harmless. They definitely are not. Taking an excess dosage can at best cause liver damage and at worst cause a long and painful death.) Dr Burn explained the procedures which were necessary and, after Luke had agreed to comply, he left Kath and me to get on with the job in hand.

Donning gloves and full-length gowns, I asked Luke to turn on to his left side before carefully passing a gastric lavage tube through his mouth and into his stomach. This may not be a particularly pleasant procedure for the patient but it is necessary to ensure that all traces of the drugs are flushed out. On the end of the tube is a large funnel and, once the tube is in place, the funnel is held down low over a bucket to allow the stomach to drain naturally. (Seeing stomach contents serves a secondary purpose – we can be sure that the tube is indeed in the stomach and not in the patient's lungs.) Once nothing further is draining out, the funnel is raised to about shoulder height and clean warm water is poured down the tube and allowed to drain into the stomach. When the funnel is empty, it is again lowered over the bucket to drain away by gravity. The procedure is repeated until the water coming back is completely clear. Depending on how much the patient has eaten or drunk beforehand, this can be a long and laborious job and it always surprises me how many overdose patients eat a large meal before attempting suicide. Perhaps psychologically it is felt to be a final meal, a last supper if you will. Thankfully, whatever the reason for doing it, it usually helps to delay the absorption of whatever drugs have been taken and sometimes saves their life.

Although considered standard treatment during the earlier part of my career, stomach wash outs could some-times be quite traumatic for the patient. The tubes were rather large and often caused the patient to gag and panic, feeling that they were about to choke. It was not unusual to have to restrain the patient gently to stop them pulling the tube out. But enforcing the wash-out procedure was increasingly coming to be recognised as a form of assault. The only other alternative was to give the patient an emetic medicine to make them vomit. If the patient refused both, they would be asked to sign a disclaimer confirming that they had refused treatment. More often than not, though, with plenty of patience and gentle persuasion the patient usually relented.

After the wash out was completed, Dr Burn returned and talked at length to Luke about his HIV diagnosis and how he was feeling. He attempted to find out what Luke had been told about the illness and tried to establish his main concerns, answering as many of his questions as he could and explaining what was likely to happen next. He listened intently as Luke unburdened himself, but it was heartbreaking to see the despair etched on the young man's face.

Anyone who was admitted into hospital after taking an overdose was first given a stomach wash out and then bloods were taken to see how much, if any, of the drug had been absorbed. Dr Burn broached the subject of taking bloods for drug and alcohol levels and warned him that, for our own personal protection, we would have to wear protective clothing. Luke was alarmed and concerned at the thought of our having to deal with his blood, knowing that it was the main source of the virus. Dr Burn smiled and assured him that we were going to be careful and that we knew what we were doing. I am certainly glad that HE knew what he was doing, because I was feeling distinctly nervous at the thought of getting a needle stick injury. However, I managed to remain calm and supported Luke's arm, keeping it steady while the doctor took the bloods. Having completed this task successfully, Dr Burn filled in the usual forms and labels before placing the specimens into two plastic bags, which he sealed and marked with a bright yellow HAZARD label on the outer bag. The purpose of this label was to alert the laboratory staff to the possibility of infection and the need for the specimens to be handled very carefully.

Luke's suicide note said that, after having watched his

friend die, he couldn't face the prospect of developing AIDS himself, but he feared mainly for his family who would no doubt have to bear an awful stigma. Knowing that Luke was clearly in a very low mental state, our next step was to advise him to seek help and support from the hospital psychiatrist.

I briefly left the room to ask the porters to take the bloods to the laboratory. After putting the specimen bags into a small box for transportation, I went to their room with it but was completely taken aback when they all refused point blank to handle the samples or take them up to the laboratory. As a group they were usually really helpful, but someone had obviously heard 'HIV' and they were now genuinely afraid to assist us. I appreciated how they felt, because of my own initial misgivings about dealing with HIV-infected blood, but I found it very difficult to believe that the specimens could still be considered dangerous when they were wrapped up inside two separate plastic bags inside another rigid container. At first I felt quite annoyed and pointedly asked them what their problem was. I tried to reassure them that they were not in any danger, but they still said no. I was wasting time standing around arguing, so I went to tell Jeanne that I was going to have to go to the laboratory myself because of the porters' refusal. I could just about understand where they were coming from, but it was frustrating that they were not even willing to listen to common sense.

When I got back, Jeanne was already talking to the porters, trying to deal with their concerns. They were not happy, though, and the question did cross my mind: what would I do if they refused to help me take Luke up to the ward? Just as I was pondering this, one of the younger porters named Andy said that he would be happy to come with me, provided he didn't have to touch anything other than the trolley.

Later, after Luke had been checked over by the psychiatrist and one of the doctors from the medical wards, Andy helped me transfer him up to a side ward on F7, where it was confirmed he was to be treated in isolation from the other patients.

I felt so sorry for Luke. He looked utterly miserable as we left him, curled up on his bed weeping. I wished him well, but he never even raised his head. As we returned, I thanked Andy for coming with me and then, as he went off back to the porters' room, I stripped the trolley down, washed it from top to bottom with antiseptic and put fresh sheets on ready for the next patient. I then placed all the used sheets in a special bag, again labelled HAZARD, and went back to work.

During basic training every nurse was taught how to deal with hazardous (i.e. highly infectious) material. The dangers of cross infection from touching anyone or anything with hands that have been in contact with infected material, faeces, urine, blood, or have even been exposed to a cough or a sneeze by an infectious patient were constantly drummed into us. Working in an isolation unit back in 1973 brought this home to me forcefully when patients had to be barrier nursed. Anyone entering the patient's room had to don surgical gloves, gown and mask. All bed linen and towels were sent to the laundry with HAZARD notices on the bag. All specimens taken were sent off to the laboratory with HAZARD labels to warn the laboratory staff. Bedpans and urinals had to be specially sterilised (before disposables were introduced), and crockery and cutlery were washed and re-used strictly within each patient's room. Everyone coming out of the isolation room had to disrobe and place their mask, gown and gloves in the HAZARD bags or bins provided within the room, before washing their hands with special antiseptic/antibacterial soap. These days, the perils of catching some exotic illness or infection are massively overshadowed by the simple dangers of poor hygiene, which can cause severe diarrhoea and vomiting, and there are vastly increasing concerns about not only HIV infection, but also Hepatitis B and Hepatitis C (both of which have become more prevalent in the population due to needle sharing among drug users, and needle stick injuries from discarded dirty needles). All of these can prove fatal. For the moment, though, it was enough to be dealing with an HIV patient. He was going to survive his attempted overdose, but we really couldn't say with confidence that he was going to be OK.

★

Throughout the evening there had been quite a number of injuries sustained due to people falling on the ice and one such patient was now waiting to be seen. An elderly lady named Grace, who was in her eighties and looked dreadfully frail and exhausted, was accompanied by her middle-aged daughter and, at first glance, it appeared that the fall had shaken her up quite badly. Her wrist was black and blue and swelling rapidly; her face and chin were full of bloodied scratches where she had hit the pavement and both her knees looked red and painful. Dr Davies examined her very gently and suggested that he have an x-ray of her wrist done to exclude the possibility of fractures.

Thankfully, her facial injuries and grazed knees were only superficial, and they looked far worse than they actually were. A thorough cleaning with antiseptic and a dry dressing on her knees to prevent her stockings from sticking to them was sufficient treatment. She was also prescribed a tetanus vaccination; though that could be given later. To be honest, Grace looked completely shattered and couldn't have cared less what treatments we gave to her. I put her arm in a sling to elevate it, in order to keep the swelling down, before ringing for a porter to take her along to X-ray in a wheelchair, accompanied by her daughter.

Fortunately the x-ray showed no bone injury, although her wrist was badly bruised and clearly very painful, so Dr Davies recommended a crêpe bandage to give it some support and suggested she keep her sling on for a further forty-eight hours until the swelling had subsided. He also prescribed a few mild analgesics to relieve her discomfort, before saying goodbye and wishing her well for the new year.

I cleaned her up as best I could before finally giving her the tetanus vaccine. Just as they were about to leave the department, her daughter quietly took me to one side and confided that she was still very concerned about her mum, who she said had been complaining recently of persistent tiredness, dizziness and shortness of breath when making the slightest exertion. She had also experienced a number of unexplained falls over the last few weeks and seemed to have lost all interest in everything around her, including a loss of appetite. When I asked the daughter if she had informed the casualty doctor or her mother's GP about any of this, she shook her head. The old lady herself had dismissed the daughter's concerns and told her not to fuss. She hadn't liked to bother the GP because he was always so busy and the casualty doctor hadn't asked. Trying to be helpful and in order to alleviate her concerns, I decided to check the old lady's blood pressure and pulse to see if they were normal, as these can often be the cause of many such symptoms. I explained to Grace what I intended to do and, although she wasn't exactly over-enthusiastic, with a little persuasion she reluctantly rolled up her sleeve and allowed me to check her out. I was greatly concerned to discover that her blood pressure was dangerously low and her pulse rate virtually non-existent. I could barely discern a faint pulse of only about thirty-eight beats per minute, when it should have been at least double that. This indicated that she was possibly in what is medically known as heart block, which basically means that her heart was not beating fast enough nor strongly enough to push sufficient blood around her body and was, in fact, in great danger of packing up altogether. It was little wonder she felt so exhausted or that she kept falling over; the old lady would probably need to have a pacemaker fitted to regulate her heart. I didn't mention this to either of them as it was not my place to do so, but I asked Grace whether it would be all right with her if I asked the doctor to make another quick check, because her blood pressure wasn't quite as good as it should be. She nodded wearily in agreement and then, before she had a chance to change her mind, I dashed off to the doctor's office.

Poor Dr Davies had just sat down with a well-earned cuppa and he screwed up his face in mock disgust when he spied me heading towards him. He stuck his tongue out at me, had a bit of a whinge about how he was unable to get even two minutes' peace and quiet, then told me not particularly politely to get lost. When I advised him about Grace's blood pressure, though, he asked me to do an immediate ECG (heart tracing) and said he would be along shortly.

At first, Grace wasn't the least bit impressed with all the fuss and really didn't want to be bothered. All she craved was to be left alone and to be allowed to go home to her bed. When I explained that her pulse was a bit slow and that was more than likely what was causing her to feel so exhausted, she resignedly agreed. With the help of a porter I put her on a stretcher and took her into resus where, assisted by her daughter, we managed to get her undressed.

When I was a student nurse we were always taught to explain any procedure to our patients first before diving in and frightening them half to death. This was one consideration my own mother also felt strongly about. She had a number of unnecessarily alarming experiences as a patient in hospital, staff simply turned up unexpectedly with a trolley full of equipment to carry out some unexplained tests. On one memorable occasion (like Grace, this was also the first time she had had a heart tracing taken), she had been so afraid that she almost vomited. A female technician dressed in a white coat simply turned up on my mum's ward pushing a large, unfamiliar machine. Stopping at the bottom of the bed she waved a form in her direction and, looking directly at Mum, asked rather abruptly what her name was. Once the woman was happy that she had found the correct patient, without so much as saying another word, she drew the curtains around the bed and started attaching metal plates to Mum's wrists and ankles. That was bad enough, but then she put several freezing cold metal suckers on to her chest before finally, and this was the worst bit, attaching long multi-coloured wires to them all before plugging the machine into the mains.

On first hearing this story, I remember laughing out loud when Mum went on to admit that she genuinely thought she was going to be given some sort of electric shock treatment. Although there was absolutely no logic to this presumption, only her fertile imagination, it serves to highlight the completely avoidable anxiety some patients experience simply because the member of staff, who after all carries out this same routine task many times each day, fails to take an extra minute or so beforehand to explain what is going to happen. On that first occasion Mum's heart was going so fast with the stress of her threatened potential electrocution that the heart tracing had to be abandoned until later in the day to give her a chance to calm down.

Bearing all that in mind, I dutifully explained the entire procedure to Grace, showing her the wires and the attachments, reassuring her that she wouldn't feel a thing. I showed her the cardiac monitor (the display looked like a small television screen) and let her watch what happened after I attached the electrodes and started the tracing. When Dr Davies came back a minute or so later to check on her, I heard him gasp in surprise as he looked at the screen, before whispering to me under his breath, 'Dear God, put her on oxygen quickly.'

Wasting no time he called the coronary care doctor and

asked him to come down urgently to Casualty; he arranged
for the radiographer to come and carry out a portable chest
x-ray; and then he put a Venflon in the back of her hand just
in case she needed urgent drugs. Dr Davies apologised to
Grace and explained briefly that she needed to be examined
by another doctor who dealt with heart patients. Poor Grace
sighed disconsolately but said nothing; she looked completely bewildered and must have wondered what on earth
was happening. One minute she was ready to go home and
the next she was attached to a machine bristling with wires,
a plastic mask over her face and having x-rays done. But she
didn't have the energy to object and simply lay back on the
pillow with her eyes tightly closed. She'd had enough and
wanted nothing more than to be allowed to sleep.

The coronary care doctor came down soon afterwards
and, after examining the heart tracing, had a quick chat to
both mother and daughter to advise them that she needed
an urgent admission to the coronary care unit to have a
pacemaker fitted. He explained in simple terms that her
heart was tired and needed a little help to control the heart
beat. Without it the rest of Grace's organs were struggling
to function properly because they were not getting the
necessary amounts of oxygen and nutrients, and that was
basically why she was feeling so tired and dizzy. He went on
to explain in detail everything which this entailed, assuring
her how much better she would feel afterwards, before
finally managing to acquire her written consent to go ahead

with the procedure. Smiling encouragingly, he then left and returned to his own unit to prepare for her arrival, but not before warning Grace that after the pacemaker had been inserted she would be bursting with energy and doing cartwheels around the hospital grounds. Her daughter smiled and thanked him, but Grace didn't seem to be listening. As soon as the doctor was ready on the ward, a porter arrived to help me take her up to the coronary care unit where the staff were all waiting to get going. After handing her over to their very capable nurses, I said my goodbyes to her, squeezed her hand tightly and wished her good luck.

When I got back to Casualty, Dr Davies, ever the gentleman, came over to me and put an arm around my shoulder to say thank you. He was quite perturbed that he had failed to pick up Grace's predicament himself, but was quick to appreciate that I had listened to her daughter and acted promptly on the information. In all fairness to him, when a patient attends Casualty with a minor injury a doctor doesn't automatically start checking their observations and asking them millions of questions about their general health and well being, especially when he or she is busy; they simply haven't got the time. The fact that the daughter felt comfortable enough and had the opportunity to approach me was the key; she had obviously been able to assess her mother's frailty at home and took the opportunity to air her concerns. Had she said nothing, Grace would probably have gone home and died very soon afterwards.

However, there wasn't to be a happy ending to this story, as it all proved to be too much for Grace, who had unfortunately left it too late for the doctors to be able to do anything to improve the situation. Despite having the pacemaker fitted, her heart was just too weak to cope and she died a few hours later. I knew from experience that without it she would have died anyway, but I still felt rather sad that she had been subjected to so much extra prodding and poking, all to no avail. Totally illogically, I felt a little guilty that it was my fault Grace had been put through so much. We always tried to do our very best to ease a patient's discomfort regardless of their age, which after all is what we were there for, but in this case we were simply too late.

Chapter 9

10.15

In the time it had taken me to transfer Grace up to the ward and get back, two more patients had been rushed into resus and both were in cardiac arrest. I popped my head around the door to let Jeanne know I was back and to see if I could be of assistance, but a brief glance confirmed the crash team were down and there were adequate numbers of staff to deal with both patients. I went back over to minor injuries and carried on with the organising and restocking of supplies. Dr Burn and Dr Pickering should have gone off duty at 10.00pm but were still busy with the cardiac arrests. Dr Davies had rapidly disappeared after handing over to Dr Cross, though, and Ann had been able to pass on the dubious privilege of being receptionist to my friend Jenny.

A few minutes later, another emergency ambulance pulled up outside with a squeal of tyres. Rather unusually all the lights were on in the rear and figures could be seen struggling as the vehicle bounced around on its suspension. The back doors suddenly burst open and a familiar face was forcibly ejected and flung several feet through the air before becoming intimate with the freezing tarmac. He was closely followed by a second, only slightly less scruffy, younger version of himself. They obviously weren't that ill or injured because, swaying and holding on to each other, both eventually managed to regain their feet before stumbling off down the road.

The staff who witnessed this little cameo performance immediately recognised the older man as 'underpants 84', one of our regulars who had been unanimously awarded this prestigious accolade by the night shift for possessing by far the most disgusting, tatty and crusty underwear seen in 1984. Despite intense competition in the intervening years from numerous candidates, he still retained the title. Although his son, who was the other 'patient' to receive flying lessons and also a Baldrick look-alike, was less well known to us, he was clearly intent on challenging his father for the championship. The ambulance crew were immediately dispatched to another emergency so were not available at the time to fill us in on what had occurred, but we later learnt that the older of the two men had sustained a small cut on his head early in the evening and his son had only then decided to call an ambulance. His injury was relatively minor but they were both extremely drunk and started fighting each other and lashing out at the senior ambulance man who was in the back of the emergency vehicle with them. U84 and his son had picked on the wrong person when they had a drunken punch-up with Vic, the senior ambulance man, though, because he was a martial arts fanatic in his spare time. But they did manage to smash two of the light bulbs in the ambulance.

About thirty minutes later Dr Pickering and some members of the crash team came out of resus looking totally dejected. Dr Pickering, in particular, appeared lost in his own thoughts and was shaking his head in despair. Normally the joker of the pack, he was always friendly and easygoing but underneath he was a sensitive and good doctor. I tentatively went over to him, thinking that one of the people in resus had perhaps been a close friend or a relative (he certainly looked as if he had lost someone very dear to him), and asked if he was OK. He simply nodded and told me that his patient had died. Although death in such cases is an everyday event in Casualty, what made this one worse, as far as he was concerned, was that the patient who had just died in cardiac arrest was Eric, the man who had been brought in earlier complaining of chest pain. Despite it having been obvious to everyone that he was very unwell, he had ignored all advice and had refused to stay in for observation and now he had paid the price with his life.

Dr Pickering had the unenviable task of informing Eric's wife, who was waiting in the relatives' room. It was one of those duties everybody hates having to carry out, especially under these particular circumstances. What a tragic waste of a life. Nevertheless, after a couple of minutes Dr Pickering regained his composure and asked Jeanne if she would accompany him to break the bad news.

His wife's wails of anguish could be heard throughout the department and, for a brief moment, everyone in the treatment area held their breath as if in respect for the bereaved woman. She was distraught with grief but, through her sobs, she was able to tell the doctor that when Eric had arrived home from Casualty earlier that evening he had been exhausted and taken himself straight to bed. He had obviously been in considerable pain and his appearance was still grey and sweaty. They'd had a massive row when she blasted him for being so pig-headed and accused him of being selfish, and not giving a thought for his young family. Seeing that this was, in fact, making him even more agitated, she left him alone to rest. After letting him sleep for a few hours she decided to take him a hot drink. Because he had closed the curtains and switched off all the lights, she flicked the bedside lamp on and went over to give him a shake but, no matter what she did, she was unable to rouse him. As panic started to set in, she put her hand on Eric's chest to check if he was still breathing, but there were few signs of life and he felt damp with perspiration. She couldn't find a pulse, so quickly telephoned for the ambulance which arrived within minutes and the crew quickly took charge of the situation.

The two ambulance men also double-checked to see if he was breathing and felt for a pulse; but there was nothing. To all intents and purposes he was dead, but they automatically commenced CPR and continued resuscitation procedures on him all the way to the hospital. The crew had no idea exactly how much time had elapsed since Eric first stopped breathing, but he was still warm and so they carried on with their efforts. Sadly, by the time they arrived at the hospital there was still no sign of a pulse; it was too late and no amount of machinery or physical intervention by the doctors helped. Eric was gone. His wife sobbed her heart out, at the same time cursing him for being such a fool and thinking that to be ill was a sign of weakness.

Anita made Dr Pickering a cup of tea, which he took into the office. Before quietly closing the door behind him, he asked to be left alone for a few minutes while he gathered his thoughts before going off duty. He was openly upset and feeling irrationally responsible because he hadn't succeeded in persuading Eric to stay in hospital earlier that evening; but it had been Eric's choice to make and he had the right to refuse help, regardless of whether or not it was the right thing to do. He chose to ignore professional advice and there was nothing more the doctor could have done. Fear is a strong emotion and each individual has to deal with it as best they can. Sadly it cost this man his life.

Over the years I have dealt with many people who have put up with considerable pain and discomfort of one sort or another for months or even years on end, ignoring it in the hope that it will go away without any sort of medical intervention. Sometimes the reason for their reluctance is simply not wishing to cause a fuss, or concluding that the problem must just be old age creeping on. At other times it is fear of the unknown that holds them back until it's too late; by the time they do ask for help, the problem is well established and too advanced for intervention or treatment. As frustrating as this may be, it is, and always will be, that person's individual choice.

My own father was a classic example; he didn't like doctors or the thought of being ill and tried to ignore any problem as much as he could. Whenever he felt unwell it was simply dismissed as a touch of flu. Many months before he died, I noticed him constantly rubbing the side of his face and he was clearly experiencing considerable pain and discomfort in his left ear, but he steadfastly refused to consult a doctor and said he probably had a bit of cold in it. As time went on, a rather unpleasant smell developed, coming from his ear, and I now believe he was afraid to seek treatment in case this confirmed his suspicions that something was seriously wrong. He had seen Mum having numerous operations over the years and he didn't want to follow suit, so he said nothing.

When my mother was dying, and his discomfort was so obviously increasing, he was then 'too busy' for several weeks to do anything about it, and no amount of persuasion was likely to change his mind. No one told Dad what to do. After Mum's death, I requested their family GP call in on him on the pretext of seeing how he was coping without her, but with the intention of giving him a check up which (after being primed) included taking a look at his ear. The doctor willingly obliged and on checking him over asked Dad how he was feeling. Dad reluctantly mentioned his ear in passing but, as soon as the doctor had a look, he was horrified to see it was a dreadfully inflamed, infected mess and referred him urgently to the ENT (Ear, Nose and Throat) surgeons at the hospital for investigation. Within days he had seen the specialist and after a number of tests and scans were carried out, he was found to have a chronic, severe infection that had actually rotted the tiny bones in his ear and had begun to infect his jaw. An urgent operation was required to try and prevent the infection spreading, but with his previous history of having suffered coronaries, the doctors were concerned that he would not cope well with the anaesthetic. It was going to be a potentially risky business whichever way they looked at it, but there was no real choice; without the operation he could die. The operation was carried out within days and appeared to go well. He was allowed home after only two days, but when I went to see him he was pouring with sweat, looked grey and miserable and once again said he had flu. I begged him to let me ring his GP but he flatly refused and although I asked him to let me stay the night, he declined my offer. I never saw my dad

alive again because during the night his condition deteriorated rapidly. He died of multiple embolisms (blood clots) to
his lungs, probably resulting from the anaesthetic and his
poor condition. A short course of antibiotics to treat the
initial minor infection in his ear could have cured him. He
was stubborn and afraid and, like Eric, it cost him his life.

While Dr Pickering had been in the relatives' room
breaking the news to Eric's wife, Dr Burn's final duty for the
evening was also to certify a death, that of the second patient
in resus; not a particularly auspicious start for the night staff.
The man, who was also in his fifties, had only just arrived at
Manchester Airport after flying over from the United States
to spend some time with his brother and his family for New
Year. According to a fellow passenger, he had complained of
feeling unwell on the plane and then, soon after collecting
his luggage from the carousel, had collapsed on the floor of
the arrivals lounge, clutching his chest. He had been rushed
to Wythenshawe by the airport ambulance (which is actually
operated by the fire-fighters based at the airport).

On arrival he was already deeply unconscious and soaking
with perspiration, his breathing was virtually undetectable
and his colouring was tinged purple/blue. However, their
first priority had been actually getting him out of the
ambulance (which was less than half the size of a normal
NHS emergency vehicle). The man was grossly overweight
and must have weighed in the region of thirty stones. The
airport stretchers were notoriously narrow and his huge

frame easily filled it, with the surplus flab spilling grotesquely over the edges. Staff couldn't even grasp hold of the sides of the trolley because they were concealed by the overhanging flesh, so trying to grip the handles was virtually impossible and vital time was wasted trying to extricate him. In the end, it took six staff to lift him out of the ambulance and transfer him on to the casualty stretcher before they managed to run him into resus. He was then unceremoniously stripped off and immediately connected to a heart monitor (which was showing a flat line) and attached to oxygen. It was pretty obvious from the moment the man arrived that there was very little sign of life, but nevertheless the crash team once again did their utmost to try to resuscitate him, but tragically it had been too late.

The next most pressing problem was establishing his identity and destination. Luckily his passport was in his jacket pocket along with his flight details and a telephone number for his relatives; all were passed on to the police. They in turn contacted the airport police who were then able to trace his brother, who was still waiting for him outside the airport arrivals hall and had seen the ambulance speed past, completely unaware what had occurred.

While all this was going on, I took a call from ambulance control alerting us of an RTA (road traffic accident) on its way involving a young man with serious leg injuries. Looking out of the window, the ambulance was already on the approach road and, although they didn't have the lights flashing, the speed at which they were travelling alerted us to the potential urgency of the patient's condition. Not too sure how bad the injuries were, Dr Cross, Chris and I waited in the stretcher area to bring the patient through. The doctor had only just come on duty and I wondered what state he would be in at 9.00am tomorrow when his eleven-hour shift ended.

Chris was about the same age as me and it was a revelation to watch her stand up to and give an ear-bashing to large drunken bruisers who were causing trouble, because she was slim and tiny and her eye line was only just above their navels! She had a couple of children to look after at home and was a confident individual – always laughing, very experienced and (like all the nurses on duty) entirely capable of coping with anything she was asked to deal with.

The patient was brought in. Michael was twenty-four and cycled everywhere, including to and from work, as he had been tonight, despite the low temperatures and the late hour. He was a keep-fit fanatic and when he wasn't cycling he spent many hours in the gym or playing squash. He couldn't understand how the driver of the lorry had failed to see him, after all he was wearing highly visible 'day-glo' cycling gear and his bike was fitted with powerful front and rear lights and had highly reflective strips all over the frame.

Of course, like every other cyclist on the road, he was resigned to riding along close to the kerb because thoughtless motorists somehow always managed to creep just that little bit too close when they were overtaking, but this time he was unlucky. A lorry was squeezing past at speed and Michael was forced to deviate as he tried to avoid a collision. Unfortunately the gutter was piled high with frozen slush and ice, and he started to slide, before losing control of his bike entirely, which sent him careering helplessly into the side of the lorry. His front wheel clipped one of the lorry's back tyres as it passed him and then, before he knew it, he had hit the carriageway hard and was helplessly cartwheeling head over heels.

When the ambulance crew brought him in, Michael was in a great deal of pain and shaking with shock. He was already being given gas and air (a mixture of fifty per cent nitrous oxide [also known as laughing gas] and fifty per cent oxygen), a medical anaesthesia that relaxes the patient and reduces the pain level. The crew had put a new, state-of-the-art inflatable splint on his leg, which had helped to stabilise what they reported was a compound fracture (which meant that the broken end of the bone had penetrated through the tissues), but they then took us completely by surprise when they asked if they could have their splint back – they had to account for every piece of equipment and they weren't allowed to leave it behind! We didn't have these up-to-date inflatable splints in Casualty so we couldn't just do a straight swap, but it seemed absolutely ridiculous to me to have to remove it, causing our patient unnecessary discomfort. I pleaded with them to let us hang on to it until he had at least been sorted out but, rules were rules, and they weren't budging an inch until they had the item back in their possession.

Looking at him more closely, our patient was of medium height with short, black, curly hair, wearing only skin-tight Lycra cycle gear and trainers. Although not very tall, he had an amazingly muscular and tanned physique that would have been the envy of many young men, but at this moment his face was as white as a sheet and he was shivering like mad, no doubt from the freezing conditions as well as shock. I reassured him that he was going to be OK but warned him that I needed to take his clothes off and change the splint on his leg. Not surprisingly, he immediately became extremely anxious and begged me not to touch his leg. I explained that the doctor needed to examine his injury thoroughly in order to assess the full extent of the damage and I promised we would be very careful not to hurt him. Michael wasn't at all convinced and implored me to leave him alone. I only wished that I felt as confident as I sounded, because I quite honestly thought it was out of order that we were being asked to disturb his leg unnecessarily.

Asking him to trust me, I put him back on gas and air and asked Chris to give me a hand. After taking in a few deep breaths, he began to relax. Chris held Michael's hand and talked to him quietly, encouraging him to carry on breathing slowly and deeply, while I started to release the air out of the splint. As it deflated I unzipped both sides so that the splint opened up like a banana skin, leaving his leg lying flat on the stretcher but still on top of the splint. Encouraging him to breathe in even deeper through the mask, after a couple more lungs full, I asked one of the ambulance men to get ready to remove the splint when I gave the word. I first took hold of the ball of his foot and ankle with my right hand and then, with my left hand placed firmly underneath his calf to support it, I slowly and carefully started to raise the leg fractionally off the stretcher, at the same time easing the ankle gently towards me to give it some traction (which would hopefully prevent Michael experiencing too much pain). As soon as the leg was lifted off the stretcher, the ambulance men were able to pull their splint out quickly and swap it with one of ours. Dr Cross came back in at just the right time and was able to check the leg rapidly before we re-splinted it and made the patient comfortable. There didn't appear to be any other serious injuries and fortunately he had been wearing a helmet, so at present all we needed to do was give him an injection of Pethadine to relieve the pain and arrange for an x-ray. There was no doubt that he had a compound fracture which was going to need urgent surgery, but the doctor needed to determine the full extent of the damage.

Before taking him to X-ray, Michael looked at us and declared, 'My God, you people really know what you are doing – I never felt a thing. Thank you.'

That was great to hear, of course, but he still looked

worried about something. He had twice started to tell me what was on his mind but then stopped; yet now he seemed to want to speak again. I closed the room door so that we could talk in private and told him to spit it out. He looked absolutely terrified, so much so that he was almost on the point of vomiting, and then he blurted out that he had been taking anabolic steroids over a long period to build up his muscles and was now scared to death that his treatment may go seriously wrong because of the drugs. Anabolic steroids are known to slow down the healing process and can cause heart and blood pressure problems, urinary and kidney problems, stunt growth in adolescents and even cause testicular shrinkage. In some cases psychological problems can also occur, such as depression and changes in mood and temper. He was obviously aware of the dangers of these drugs but, like so many others, he never thought that anything could ever happen to him. Surgery under general anaesthetic could be problematic for him but was unavoidably necessary due to the nature and extent of his injuries.

Michael begged me not to tell his family, because they would be so ashamed that he was taking these drugs, but I was far more concerned that the doctors should be informed. I advised him that I had no choice but to let the doctors know. He acknowledged and accepted this. I had a quick word with Dr Cross, who went back to speak to him and pointed out that whatever was said would, of course, be treated in confidence, as far as his family and friends were concerned, but that all the doctors and nurses who were caring for him would have to be given this additional information.

Michael's x-rays were taken and came back showing a number of particularly nasty fractures. He had shattered his tibia and fibula in several places (the two bones in his lower leg) and was going to have to undergo extensive surgery. He was liable to be in hospital for many weeks, not least because the steroids would very likely impede his progress.

Dr Cross rang the orthopaedic doctor on call who came down to Casualty and, after informing his superior, arranged to admit him on to the ward prior to going to theatre. He had a quiet word with the ward nurses on duty about the lad's anabolic steroids use and warned them that his family were unaware of this. We then contacted Michael's family to tell them of his whereabouts, before Chris took him up to the ward.

Half an hour later, Jeanne suddenly realised that she hadn't seen Chris for quite a long time. Checking around the different areas, she asked if anyone had seen her recently and Theresa suggested she might be in cas obs, but there was no sign of her. After finally checking the staff room, plaster theatre and ladies toilets, Jeanne popped into the porters' room and was informed that Chris had gone with Fred, one of the porters, to take Michael up to orthopaedics about twenty minutes earlier. A quick call to the ward confirmed that, although expected, neither she nor the patient had yet arrived, so one of the other porters was dispatched to retrace their footsteps.

Barry, another of our long-serving porters who had gone searching for her, came back about ten minutes later with a big smile on his face to report that all three were stuck in the lift and the fire brigade were on their way after being alerted by a passing member of staff. Michael was a little claustrophobic apparently and started to have a panic attack, so Chris had her hands full trying to pacify him but was also feeling guilty because we had now been left short-staffed in Casualty on such a potentially busy night. Fred, on the other hand, was perfectly happy to get an unexpected break. I think the prospect of imminent rescue by a hunky fireman kept Chris's spirits up, although she was in there for nearly an hour before emerging looking thoroughly dishevelled. Thankfully, the patient was fine and thought it would make an amusing story to tell his family.

One or two of the lifts at Wythenshawe were notoriously temperamental, even though they were maintained on a regular basis. I tried to avoid them myself as far as possible, although they were far superior to the monstrosities we used at Blackburn Royal Infirmary when I was a young trainee. Almost inevitably I found myself stuck in one with a patient when I was about eighteen years old. Thankfully the patient was not desperately ill and we weren't in there for long because the engineer arrived within a couple of minutes. Being claustrophobic myself, it wasn't a very pleasant experience, especially when, in my case, the door opened fully at one stage and I was confronted by a solid brick wall. After that little adventure I was terrified of lifts and have to admit shamefacedly that on one occasion, when I was taking a patient from the ward down to X-ray, I pushed the lady into the lift, pressed the button for the ground floor and then ran like hell down the stairs to meet the lift at the bottom. The patient, who had her back to the lift door, was still chatting away to me, completely unaware that I had not actually been in the lift with her. I never owned up or told anyone else what I had done but I felt absolutely dreadful about it for a long time afterwards. I never repeated that trick and still cringe whenever I think about it. Matron would have sacked me, and quite rightly so.

Chapter 10

10.45pm

Back in minor injuries, our little box of admission cards was almost empty once again, but if Theresa and I were hoping for a few quiet moments, we were to be sorely disappointed. No sooner had we cleared the decks, when in came Helen, another of our regulars, who arrived by ambulance. Within moments, the noise levels in the department had risen by several decibels.

There was a collective groan when we saw her being helped down the ambulance steps and escorted through to reception by two police officers, because everyone who had any previous experience of her knew that she was a walking disaster area. A large, blousy young woman with both a personality disorder and a drink problem, she was commonly known for self-harming. She would habitually slash herself with any sharp object that she could lay her hands on, and it was far from unusual to see her in Casualty several times in the same week. Her arms, chest, breasts and abdomen were a mass of unsightly scar tissue and, at some stage in the past she had even cut off one of her nipples with a pair of scissors. Helen was a fighter and could be aggressive and extremely violent, depending on the amount of alcohol she had consumed and whether or not she was allowed to get her own way. Treated carefully, however, she could be a real pussy cat.

She staggered along and, as usual, was shouting, swearing and expecting to be seen at once. According to the accompanying police officers, she had been thrown out of her local pub for being drunk, then subsequently arrested soon afterwards for affray. Her arms had gaping wounds where she had slashed them with a broken bottle and there was a trail of blood from the ambulance bay to reception because she had already ripped off the dressings and bandages put on by the ambulance crew.

Recognising me immediately, she shouted cheerfully across the corridor, 'Hi Joan. I've cut my f**king wrists, luv. Will you stitch 'em for me?'

Because she had been to Casualty so often, she knew all the nurses by their Christian names. One morning when Jeanne was out shopping, she heard a loud voice shouting her name above the noise of heavy traffic across a busy main road. As she turned and looked up, she saw Helen weaving her way through the moving vehicles, greeting her like a long-lost relative. Pretending to be in a hurry, Jeanne made her excuses and a rapid exit, praying that no one who might recognise her thought they could possibly be friends. Helen, who was already quite drunk (or more probably still drunk from the night before), waved her off happily, promising to call into Casualty again soon.

People like Helen kept us busy in the suture room. In other Casualty departments where I had worked, the nurses were never given the opportunity to stitch wounds, but here in Wythenshawe Hospital it was an essential part of the job, due to the sheer volume of lacerations we dealt with every day. All trained nurses were expected to carry out their share of this task because it allowed the doctors to carry on and deal with the more serious cases. I thoroughly enjoyed the challenge of suturing, which was quite ironic because at home it takes me a lifetime to so much as stitch on a shirt button. But to me it was an art that could mean the difference between the patient being left permanently scarred or not.

The strict protocol we were obliged to follow stated that the patient had to be thoroughly examined by a doctor first, to ascertain the full extent of any damage. If the wound was superficial then the nurses were allowed to do the suturing, but deeper lacerations had to be deferred to the doctors.

Helen was initially put in a cubicle on the minor injuries side and Dr Cross greeted her with his trademark warm and friendly smile. Within seconds she was putty in his hands. After cursorily examining her arms, he asked why she had hurt herself. She shrugged her shoulders and lowered her head, clearly unable or unwilling to get into that conversation. He walked her round to the suture room where she permitted him to examine her wounds more thoroughly; checking how deep the cuts were and trying to establish whether she had damaged any tendons or ligaments. She appeared to be totally at ease, grinning and fluttering her eyelashes at the doctor, telling him what a nice young man he was. Dr Cross was nobody's fool, though, and, having already dealt with her on a number of previous occasions over the last few months, knew exactly how to handle her. After establishing that Helen's wounds were, in fact, only superficial, he asked me (with a huge smile on his face) to do the honours, and then made his getaway while the going was good.

As I turned around to set up the trolley and sort out the required instruments, she started cursing loudly when she saw the two officers still waiting for her in the corridor outside and decided to make a dash for freedom. Jumping off the stretcher she legged it straight for the nearest exit, but hadn't got very far before she tripped over her own feet and fell heavily on the floor.

The policemen went to help her up and try to prevent her from hurting herself further, but were rewarded for their efforts by Helen spitting and attempting to bite a chunk out of one of the officer's legs. It was agreed between us that it was probably safer to stitch her up where she was on the floor, since that way she at least couldn't fall off the stretcher and break an arm or a leg. So, not for the first time, I ended up stitching Helen while kneeling on the floor alongside her in the corridor with two policemen holding her down for her own safety.

A number of people who were sitting outside the suture room waiting patiently for their own turn to be stitched stared in disbelief as this little scenario unfolded in front of them, shaking their heads in disgust at the sheer volume of foul language coming out of her mouth (having said that, many of them were completely in their element, watching our fracas with an intense morbid fascination). One or two even offered expressions of sympathy for us having to put up with such a carry on, despite Helen telling them all to 'Mind your own f**king business' and kicking out in their general direction to reinforce her point.

Jeanne came to see what was going on but, when she saw who it was we had spread-eagled on the floor, she certainly didn't hang around very long. Instead, she smirked, nodded in my direction and half-heartedly inquired if I needed any help, and then promptly disappeared before I had the chance to say yes.

A minute or so later, two ambulance men brought in another stretcher case and they both winked at me as they passed by, watching our largely unsuccessful efforts to stop Helen rolling around with great amusement. Wishing us luck, they quickly settled their gentleman on to the stretcher in the overdose room before carefully squeezing past us to get to reception to book in their patient. Like us, they were all too familiar with Helen's belligerent mood swings and had no intention of getting involved if they could avoid it.

Once I had managed to put a firm dressing on her wounds, I helped Helen to her feet and walked with her back to the police van, where she actually hugged me and whispered in a childish voice that she quite liked the look of the doctor who had examined her and wouldn't mind seeing him again. I shuddered at the thought. Before assisting her into the back of the van, I asked her to promise me that she would be on her best behaviour when she arrived at the police station. I must admit this was more in hope than expectation.

It must have only been about fifteen minutes or so later when we received a call from Brownley Road nick asking apologetically if it would be OK to bring Helen back. She had been passing the time by pulling out her stitches and had thrown all the dressings on the cell floor. We couldn't very well refuse, but I jokingly warned Dr Cross that it was entirely his fault because he had been far too nice to her and that she was almost certainly on the pull. For some reason, the thought of Helen offering her body to him on a plate didn't fill him with unbridled passion!

We could have done without the aggravation but, a short time after their phone call, the police van pulled up outside again. Helen emerged from the back in handcuffs and minus her shoes (she had obviously been up to her regular party trick of using their shins for penalty practise) but, unusually for her, she was looking rather sheepish. She grinned when she saw me waiting for her and actually said that she was sorry, before putting her head down in an unconvincing pretence that she was ashamed of her behaviour (which must have been a first, I suppose). You never know, though, especially since by this time she just might have been beginning to sober up.

The very first thing she did was to ask if the same young doctor would be coming to see her; the minx really had done it simply to see Dr Cross again! I took her by the arm and led her once again to the suture room, warning her that she had better behave herself because there would not be a third time. Dr Cross reluctantly came to see her, but this time spoke very matter-of-factly, making sure that he kept a safe distance. He examined Helen carefully for a second time, checking that her wounds were no worse than they had been previously and told her quite firmly that he would not see her again if she persisted in being so juvenile. She apologised once more, giggled like a young schoolgirl and waved to Dr Cross as he left the room.

On the whole, I have to admit that when Helen was being stitched she rarely caused trouble and was generally quite well behaved. She never bothered to have a local anaesthetic because she was so used to having stitches that she had become immune to the discomfort (mind you, the alcohol in her system usually acted as a pretty good pain killer anyway). Sometimes she would even point out where she would like us to place her stitches, and seemed quite content to watch with a sort of detached fascination as we worked. On this occasion, she appeared to be cooperating well and even seemed relatively placid; that is, until Tony came in to say hello. The patient who had been brought into the overdose room when Helen and the three of us had been struggling on the floor, turned out to be an acquaintance of hers and was yet another of our regular patients. Having sobered up quite a lot by this time, Tony was now only moderately drunk and had already been given some medicine to make him vomit the tablets he claimed to have swallowed. While everyone was waiting for this treatment to take effect, he had heard Helen's voice and had sneaked out of his room (still carrying a bucket in readiness) to remonstrate with the two officers accompanying her, demanding that she be released immediately. He was warned in no uncertain terms to mind his own business, while Wendy and Kath did their best to get him back into the overdose room and away from Helen. All went quiet for a short time and I was able to re-suture Helen's wounds successfully and replace her dressings. As soon as she was back on her feet and had been handcuffed, though, it began to sink in that she wasn't going anywhere except back to the cells. When she started cursing, swearing and shouting for help, her tipsy friend again loomed in the doorway of the suture room and repeated his demand that the officers free the Wythenshawe One. He was given a final warning that he, too, would be arrested if he didn't go away and keep quiet. To avoid any further trouble they decided to return Helen to the cells as swiftly as they could.

Not to be ignored, Tony followed them outside to the police van where he tried to drag one of the officers off her physically, which in turn sent Helen into a frenzy of activity. Kicking out with all her strength, she tried her utmost to get away from the second officer, who was by now holding on to her for dear life. Every loitering drunk and passer-by in the area stopped to watch the free-for-all, most of them laughing and shouting encouragement to Helen as the participants in this pantomime continued to bounce around the car park. When some semblance of order had been restored, Helen was carted off back to the cells and her new best friend (complete with bucket) was 'persuaded' to go back into his room. The van rapidly disappeared down the road, rocking dangerously from side to side as she threw herself around inside the vehicle. If she wasn't black and blue with bruises in the morning I would be amazed, but by then she would probably have little recollection how she acquired them.

I sometimes (admittedly not very often) felt quite sorry for Helen because she was a demandingly complex young woman, liable to transform her character in the blink of an eye. She seemed completely alone at times and yet never lost an opportunity to chat up any unsuspecting man who she considered might conceivably fancy her, rather like Dr Cross (who was teased mercilessly and relentlessly by the staff during the remainder of his rotation in Casualty for being on Helen's hit list of potential suitors).

There was one memorable occasion, soon after I had started working at Wythenshawe, when Helen had taken a particular fancy to a middle-aged man sitting in the waiting room quietly minding his own business. In staggered Helen, drunk and almost incapable of standing unaided. Quickly scanning the other waiting patients, for some reason she made a beeline for this poor, unsuspecting gent, who was far more interested in trying to solve his crossword puzzle than searching for a soul mate. He looked totally panic-stricken as she plonked herself down beside him, almost landing in his lap. Her chat-up technique needed a little work, though, since she smiled beguilingly at her quivering victim and hoisted her blouse up to her chin, shouting at the top of her voice, 'Do you want to see my tits?'

The other waiting patients were shocked into almost total silence as she unveiled massive unfettered breasts dangling helplessly over her equally large, flabby belly. One or two brave people told her to behave and cover up; others smirked and thought it was hilarious, although they would no doubt have rapidly changed their minds if she'd turned her attention on them. The man was severely embarrassed and didn't know where to look as she thrust her heaving chest under his nose. Blushing furiously, he jumped to his feet and rushed outside in a vain attempt to escape her clutches.

Watching all this was really quite alarming and, although we were so used to her antics by now, she had gone too far this time. However, she hadn't finished yet. Not wanting to lose her intended paramour, she was soon heading after him and continued to make a complete nuisance of herself. Sister went to the man's assistance and tried to distract Helen by asking her if there was a reason she had come to Casualty that evening or whether she was waiting for someone, only to be told in no uncertain terms to mind her own business. It appeared that she was simply socialising and had no intention of being moved on. When Sister then asked her to leave the department, Helen became increasingly abusive and the police had to be called to have her removed.

Several officers arrived promptly to help out, but their faces said it all when they saw who it was they were being asked to eject, knowing full well that there was no way that she would go quietly. Helen screamed like a banshee when she saw them come through the doors and her language was x-rated. The policemen who knew her best nearly always tried the softly, softly approach first; despite knowing full well what the inevitable response will be.

Looking at each policeman individually, she slowly eyed them up and down with undisguised contempt and screamed at the top of her voice, 'I've HAD every single one of these bastards in the back of their van!'

I glanced fleetingly at the officer nearest to me and whispered, 'And there's me thinking I was your only true love.'

The look he gave me was priceless, but he didn't get the chance to respond before Helen tried to do a runner and then it was all systems go as she (literally) kicked off. They carried out a pincer movement with two officers coming up from behind and taking hold of her arms, while at the same time another officer quickly removed her shoes before she could maim him for life. They then ran her backwards to the waiting police vehicle (to keep her slightly off balance and prevent her kicking them) and 'helped' her inside, the van rocking violently as she attempted to trash the interior and attack the officers. I could only imagine the chaos at the other end when they arrived at the cells that night.

Now that Helen had left again this time, all was reasonably quiet – which was most unusual. But the night was still young and, presumably, the people still getting ready for their big New Year's Eve parties had better things to do than wait around in Wythenshawe Casualty Department.

There were two stretcher patients still to be dealt with, one being an asthmatic who was being looked after by Kath; and the other was Tony, Helen's friend, who Wendy was sorting out. After first claiming to have taken an overdose, he had swiftly changed his story when the doctor told him he would need to have a stomach wash out. He then confessed to returning home drunk earlier that night and being thrown out by his long-suffering wife. She had locked the door and told him not to return until he had sobered up. In his drunken stupor he had decided that 'those nice nurses and doctors' in Casualty would, if he was lucky, provide him with a cup of tea. The trouble was, all the nice nurses and doctors had met him too many times before under similar circumstances. We had long ago come to realise that we couldn't believe a word he said. Knowing how often he told lies, and not really being able to ascertain whether he had actually taken any drugs or not, the doctor insisted that, no matter what he said, he had to have his stomach emptied one way or another.

Having been given a wash out in the past, he didn't much care for that, thank you very much, but eventually agreed to have his usual 'black medicine', which was an oral emetic liquid (a medicine that would make the patient vomit within about twenty to thirty minutes, hopefully thus emptying the stomach contents). After all, he didn't mind being sick and it was freezing outside and he still needed somewhere to shelter for the night. Patients knew full well that, to avoid being accused of negligence, the doctors would have to err on the side of caution and check them out fully. Blood tests would also have to be carried out, but he didn't mind those either, and that would mean even more time indoors rather than out in the bitterly cold night.

The doctor grudgingly took blood samples to test for drug levels and prescribed the oral medicine. Tony was perfectly happy providing we didn't put 'that tube' into his stomach. He was placed on a chair in the overdose room clutching a large bucket and had been sitting quietly waiting for something to happen when Helen had kicked off outside.

After his little encounter with the forces of law and order, he settled down in his seat again to await developments and, sure enough, a short time later the sounds of him throwing up echoed around the department. As it turned out, he'd taken nothing more lethal than substantial volumes of alcohol, but he had achieved his objective and managed to pass an hour or two hanging around Casualty. He wasn't usually aggressive to the nurses (although he hated the police) and cooperated well with the staff, but he was a nuisance who, along with others like Helen, continued to drain countless thousands of pounds each year from hospital resources.

While I had been away sorting out Helen in the suture room, Theresa had been struggling along capably on her own in the treatment area. As I was making my way back to continue helping her with the minor injuries, I couldn't help but notice that there were even more police officers wandering around and she was looking a little flustered. A slim diminutive figure, Theresa was a quiet, hard-working nurse who was married to one of the theatre orderlies at the hospital. Experienced and used to dealing with drunken patients as a matter of course, Theresa had encountered a problem which needed Jeanne's intervention. Two brothers had come to the treatment area after one of them sustained a cut to his head in a brawl outside a pub, which the doctor said needed stitches. Both were drunk and had been forcefully instructed to extinguish the cigarettes they insisted on smoking in the cubicle. The uninjured brother had objected and went off into the sluice room, where he barricaded the door and continued smoking and drinking from a bottle concealed in his pocket. Despite all Theresa's repeated requests, he refused to come out. Instead, he goaded her through the small window in the sluice door, by giving her a V-sign and flicking his cigarette at the wall behind him. Jeanne was having none of it, particularly because of the dangers of a fire should his cigarette butt lodge among the disposable bedpans stored in the sluice, so she summoned the police once again. Even when the police officers arrived, though, he still refused to open the door and continued smoking, drinking, swearing and spitting. Eventually, with assistance from a couple of porters, they forced the door open and dragged the mindless idiot out in handcuffs to be charged with being drunk and disorderly. After being stitched up, the other brother who was equally troublesome was turfed out, too, and spent the night sobering up in the adjoining cell.

I have always been particularly aware of the dangers posed by discarded cigarette butts after a patient at Blackpool caused a ward to be evacuated. After sneaking into the sluice for an illicit fag one night, this man heard someone approaching and flicked away the glowing stub before going back to bed. The embers smouldered for some time before a pile of disposable items caught fire and all the patients, some of them bedridden and on traction with broken limbs, had to be evacuated down the fire escape. The damage, thankfully, was fairly minimal but the consequences could have been very serious indeed.

Chapter 11

11.30pm

We now had a fairly steady stream of walking wounded wandering in through the door and the box of casualty cards for minor injuries was being constantly topped up by the receptionist. Jenny worked a permanent night shift rota in Casualty from 10.00pm to 9.00am, seven nights on duty and seven nights off, a pattern which allowed her plenty of flexibility to spend time with her son as she was bringing him up. Together with Wendy, the three of us were good friends. Jenny and I had been matrons of honour at Wendy's wedding to Trevor a couple of summers ago, the same year our two families had been on holiday together to Minorca. Jenny looked forward to her annual breaks in the sun and enjoyed holidaying with Jeanne from time to time, too. Perhaps even more than the other night staff, dealing with abusive and drunken behaviour was water off a duck's back for the receptionist in Casualty, and Jenny very rarely let the provocation get to her; although you will always get the odd one.

When I went along to the waiting room to round up our next victims, I called out eight names and the patients promptly formed an orderly queue and then made their way into the treatment area. Wendy, who was now working with me, organised them into their cubicles but there appeared to be one patient missing. The last person hadn't responded so, after I had called out his name several more times without success, Jenny came through from reception to point him out. We both had to smile at the vision of serenity sprawled in front of us. Bernard, a middle-aged man, was slumped precariously over the side of a hospital wheelchair, deeply asleep and snoring his head off. Jenny ruefully informed us that some passing Samaritan had called for an ambulance after finding him face down in the gutter outside a pub. By the looks of him, he had obviously been in some form of recent altercation. His lip was cut and he had a rapidly swelling black eye. At present, though, he was completely oblivious to the world. Not surprising really, seeing as the landlord of the pub where our dozy patient was a regular patron told the ambulance crew that Bernard (a known alcoholic) had been in his hostelry since lunchtime knocking back pints and chasers like they were going out of fashion. At some point later in the evening, he was reported to have seriously insulted one of his fellow drinkers who, most unfortunately for him, was built like a rather large brick outhouse and had taken mortal offence to Bernard's drunken comments. After receiving a good, old-fashioned smack in the mouth, our sleeping beauty had been thrown out on to the street, where he was eventually found hugging the pavement.

Looking at him from a safe distance, I estimated that he stood no more than five feet tall and he reminded me of a grumpy little garden gnome who had hurt himself falling off a toadstool. His coarse, weather-beaten face was bruised and bleeding, and he looked like a badly wrapped Christmas present. He was wearing an old, moth-eaten jacket that had definitely seen better days and stank of booze and cigarettes; most of the buttons were missing and the sleeves were at least a couple of inches too short. On the other hand, his trousers looked fairly new but were several sizes too big for him, necessitating the use of a thick leather belt to keep them aloft, with massive turn-ups on both legs that had ridden up and were now comically hanging at half-mast just below his knees. All he needed was a green pointy hat with a bell on top and a fishing rod to complete the picture. This sorry-looking specimen was completely and utterly bladdered.

I looked at Jenny and grinned, 'Only a mother could love him.'

The ambulance crew who had brought him in had assessed his injuries as best they could and decided that he was not seriously hurt, so they had propped him up in the waiting room before booking him in at reception and remanding him into our tender care.

It was just my luck to win the booby prize, so I asked Anita, our helper, if she would give me a hand to help steer Bernard into minor injuries. She was a genuinely kind and caring lady, who kept chatting away to Bernard, smiling and laughing and generally trying her best to establish contact with him through the fog of alcohol, although the little hobbit kept nodding off, grunting and snuffling in his slumbers. He was now out for the count and no amount of shaking seemed to make any sort of impression, his snores reverberating around the department like rolls of thunder, but at least this performance was providing a bit of light relief for the other individuals sitting around in the waiting area, as several people joined in as I shouted his name in a desperate attempt to rouse him. I was just beginning to worry that he had received a particularly hard punch, or banged his head more seriously than we first thought, when he started to come out of his drunken stupor and became extremely aggressive, lashing out with his clenched fists as if in a boxing ring. Not to be put off, and realising that he was, in fact, scarcely capable of knocking the skin off a rice pudding, I took a firm grip on the back of his collar to make sure that he couldn't fall forwards off the wheelchair on to his face, while Anita held on to his dangling legs, and we unceremoniously wheeled him backwards down the corridor. The unexpected movement of the chair swinging around the corners seemed to rouse him completely from his reverie and he gripped the arms of the wheelchair as if his life depended on it, screaming for help at the top of his voice. In all fairness, he must have wondered why the earth had suddenly started to move in the wrong direction, and it took him a minute or two to get his bearings. It was highly amusing watching the puzzled look on his face slowly alter, as he tried desperately to figure out where he was, jerking around and striking out like a marionette on the end of his string, beady little eyes puffy and bloodshot from the booze.

Wendy burst out laughing when she saw me dragging him in. 'Did they not have one in full size then?' she said quietly, with a big smile on her face.

Before I could say anything, Bernard frowned and spat out a barely intelligible, foul-mouthed tirade as he tried to get up out of the wheelchair and launch himself at her. The image of him trying his utmost to stand up was hilarious, bearing in mind that I was still holding on to the back of his collar (albeit with only one finger) – his arms were flailing around and his legs were pedalling like a hamster on a treadmill. Thankfully, no matter how hard he tried, he just didn't have enough momentum to get to his feet and couldn't for the life of him understand why. As he continued to rock frantically backwards and forwards, swearing his head off, I didn't dare release my grip. In his present state, one really violent movement could easily have seen him face down on the deck and then I would probably have found myself being sued. So, although I had plenty of other jobs I could have been getting on with, I had to stay with Bernard until the doctor had checked him out (for some unfathomable reason, Wendy didn't seem very keen to swap places with me).

The patients waiting in the other cubicles were straining to see what all the noise was about and had a good laugh at his antics, but this only incensed Bernard even more. As luck would have it, by the time Dr Cross arrived, he had tired himself out and was nodding off again, which made it much easier to examine him without causing another full-blown battle.

From the state of his clothing, it was plain to see that Bernard had been bleeding quite heavily from his mouth (all mouth injuries, even minor ones, tend to bleed profusely) and a witness had said that she had seen him strike the back of his head on the pavement quite hard when he went down; though no one could say whether he had actually lost consciousness. So, bearing this history in mind, the way he was behaving was not necessarily due entirely to alcohol. Head injuries can sometimes cause restlessness and aggression, especially if the patient has a fractured skull or a clot on the brain, and it was therefore vital to rule these out.

Dr Cross tentatively checked Bernard thoroughly from head to toe, feeling around his head for any obvious lumps, cuts and bleeding, while I carried out all the usual routine observations for head injuries, i.e. checking his consciousness level, blood pressure, pulse, temperature and pupil reactions; all of which were normal. When the doctor tried to sit him forward to check the back of his head and the inside of his ears, all hell broke loose as Bernard once again sprang to life. He remained totally uncooperative and was still incapable of stringing more than two words together, but he renewed his futile attempts to flatten anyone and everyone within swinging distance. Although I was now hanging on to him as hard as I could, he was squirming and sliding around on the wheelchair as if he had Vaseline on his backside.

Examining his mouth was simply a bridge too far. There was no way that Dr Cross or I were going to risk putting our fingers anywhere near his rotten discoloured teeth, and when the doctor ventured close enough to try and get him to open his mouth, Bernard snapped at him like a rabid dog. No amount of gentle persuasion or firm reasoning was going to do the trick; he was simply too drunk to comply. It was still essential that we finish checking him out thoroughly, though, so this part of the examination would have to wait until later. In the interim, it was imperative that he had x-rays to make sure he didn't have any skull or facial fractures, and these tests were treated as a priority.

From his appearance he had taken quite a beating, but we were going to need much more cooperation from him if we were going to do our jobs properly. The best solution would have been for someone to sit with him while he sobered up sufficiently to comply with the examination, but it didn't take a mastermind to realise that this wasn't really an option – we didn't have enough staff to spare one to babysit a drunk. In the end, I was 'volunteered' to accompany him to the X-ray department while they had the pleasure of his company.

Anita had been called back to help out on the stretcher side and all the porters must have been busy (at least there wasn't one to be found anywhere), so taking a deep breath I decided to take him by myself. As I set off down the corridor towards X-ray, in my wisdom I thought it might be safer for Bernard if I stood directly in front of him with my hands on either arm of the wheelchair, pushing him backwards. In this way I could keep an eye on him and steer the chair at the same time, while hopefully preventing him from collapsing forwards. I should have had more sense, of course, and it certainly proved not to be my brightest idea because the first thing he did when we turned the corner was to nearly break his neck in an attempt to give me a Glasgow kiss. Luckily I was a little too quick for him and, just in the nick of time, I dodged out of the way. The surprise of his attack must have made me give out a little yelp as his forehead missed my nose by a fraction of an inch, and Sister came running into the corridor to see what was happening. Although momentarily startled, I rapidly regained my grip on the back of his collar and managed to drag him back upright in the chair, and then threatened to have him locked up if he tried it again. His response to this was a surprisingly clear and precise request that I 'F**k off.' That was the final straw for Jeanne who telephoned for the police.

As fortune would have it, there was a patrol car passing and two of the local officers walked in only minutes later. Sister told them what had happened and, after pointing to the culprit, asked them if they would assist the patient to X-ray. Big Daft Denis was at least six feet three inches tall and his partner Peter was much the same size, and when they stood shoulder to shoulder they tended to block out the natural light. Their sheer presence was normally enough to intimidate most people, but not our drunken little friend Bernard. As soon as he eyeballed the pair, he became even more defiant and put up his fists to challenge them to a fight. They both found it highly amusing that he fancied his chances against the pair of them but managed to resist the challenge and, speaking very politely (in order to avoid antagonising him further), advised him that he was going to be taken to X-ray to assess whether his injuries were serious. Then they warned him, in no uncertain terms, not to start any more trouble. Denis grabbed hold of his legs to stop him from kicking out and Peter held both arms firmly by his sides so, with me still hanging on to the back of Bernard's collar, we succeeded in pushing and dragging his wheelchair safely to X-ray without any further bloodshed. The two of them promised to stay with me to make sure I was safe and that he behaved himself.

Denis and Peter were also members of the GMP Tactical

Aid Group (known as the Tag team, which was the squad of officers who were used to police large crowd control situations and potentially violent confrontations) so we were always delighted to see them at such times. Denis generally went about his job with a huge grin on his face (hence his nickname) and very little managed to dent his sunny disposition. I had nothing but admiration for all the Wythenshawe police officers, who were always absolutely brilliant in the support they gave us. Not having our own security staff, they never hesitated to come to our assistance if we were in trouble and they saved us from assault on an almost daily basis. They turned up quickly and willingly and, as far as the nurses in Casualty were concerned, they were the best.

It turned out that Bernard was well known to the two officers, who had arrested him on countless previous occasions. They knew only too well just how nasty he could be when he was drunk, which, according to them, seemed to be occurring more and more frequently. What followed next, though, was like a sketch from a Benny Hill comedy.

Once we had managed to get him into the x-ray room we still needed to get him physically up on to the x-ray table. We tried our best to make him understand what we wanted him to do and asked him to help us, but there was no way on earth that he was going to cooperate and he completely ignored all our requests. It was eventually decided that, for his own safety, he should be lifted on to the table bodily. This was, of course, no problem for the two large coppers, who picked him up like a bag of feathers; but keeping him immobile during the procedures was a totally different ball game. Arms and legs were flicking about in every direction, so we didn't dare leave him alone in case he fell off the table. He still fought and rolled about, even when we weren't touching him but only standing close by, so we knew there was no way he would remain still long enough for us to take the x-rays. There was nothing else for it; the radiographer suggested that we all put on lead jackets to protect ourselves from radiation exposure and hold on to him as best we could for as long as possible.

Not surprisingly, most of the x-rays had to be taken several times and, by the time we had finished, all three of us were sweating heavily and feeling absolutely exhausted. However, the x-rays were eventually processed successfully and we returned to Casualty without any further major incident. Dr Cross studied the films to determine what our next course of action should be. Thankfully, the x-rays were all clear and Bernard's head injury observations were still normal when we checked them again later. This was especially good news because, as far as the doctor and therefore the hospital were concerned, Bernard was now fit to be discharged. The only problem still to be addressed was what to do with him next. He was far too drunk to be allowed to walk home on his own and would probably have ended up falling over and breaking a leg or getting mown down by a car. During the night shift, there were only emergency ambulances on duty and these were few and far between and not to be used as taxis. Bernard didn't have any money in his pockets for us to get him a real taxi and, in any event, no one was even sure where he lived. We couldn't keep him in hospital because, apart from being inebriated, there was little wrong with him that warranted a hospital bed and, like the ambulances, there were few available.

However, as fate would have it, while we were pondering what to do with him, he started swearing and once again lashed out at one of the officers. That confirmed his destiny; it was decided to give him a bed for the night in the cells and he was promptly arrested for being drunk and disorderly.

He still wouldn't let us check the inside of his mouth, though, so we handed out routine head injury instructions to the officers, advising them what symptoms to watch out for, and told them to bring him back if they were at all concerned. They called for the van to take him back to the police station to sleep it off and, although Bernard was a little reluctant to get in at first, he cheered up when Denis told him the custody sergeant only wanted to wish him Happy New Year.

Chapter 12

After struggling on the floor with Helen and messing about with Bernard, my hair and cap were all over the place again and my makeup definitely needed a little reconstructing here and there. When I finally got a few minutes to myself, I sneaked off to the changing room to tidy up and took the opportunity to nip out to the car park to collect my party food from the boot. As usual, the staff all appeared to have gone overboard with their food, some of which had already been set out, and it looked so good that I was quite looking forward to getting stuck in, although any more mince pies would probably finish me off after the last few days.

I had just got back to the department after handing my culinary contributions over to Anita (who as our resident catering queen was in charge of organising the buffet), when I heard the unmistakeable warble of the trimphone coming from the treatment area. The trimphone is the direct emergency telephone link from Manchester Airport to Casualty and it only ever rings when there is the possibility of an impending major incident. I rushed straight back to the treatment area where a few of the other nurses were already gathered, looking at each other in expectant silence as Jeanne hurried over to answer the call. All eyes were on Jeanne's face, watching her expression intently as she listened very carefully to what the caller had to say, before eventually replacing the receiver and turning to us with a resigned expression on her face.

She took a deep breath and said, 'The pilot of an incoming flight has informed air traffic control that he can't be positive the plane's undercarriage is down and locked because the warning light on the flight deck is refusing to light up. He and his copilot have gone through all their standard checks several times but still can't get an indication confirming that the landing gear is actually down. As a precaution we have been put on standby, along with all the other emergency services, in case they are obliged to make a forced landing.'

In my imagination I could see all the passengers blissfully sitting there with their seatbelts on getting ready to land, happy to be home in time for the New Year celebrations. I was sure that they were completely unaware of any potential problems their pilots were experiencing, but I confess to feeling very glad I wasn't up there with them. Despite having flown many times without so much as experiencing even minor turbulence, I am invariably like a coiled spring every time I go on board and then can't wait to get off. My stomach did somersaults at the mere thought of potential disaster.

The slightest hint of a problem on board any flight is, of course, always taken very seriously by pilots and their air traffic controllers, therefore such alerts to the emergency services are actually not that uncommon. Thankfully, in the vast majority of cases, the problem proved to be nothing more untoward than a faulty warning light, but for everyone's safety nothing was ever left to chance. At present, the pilots of the plane had been asked to reduce height to make a pass over the runway to see if the air traffic controllers in the tower could spot whether the wheels were down or not.

No matter how many times we were put on alert, until we received a second call giving us the all clear, we remained on tenterhooks; however, we had to carry on treating patients as usual, all the while listening out expectantly for an update.

I checked around to see where I was most needed, and took over from Theresa who, having been on duty the day of the Manchester air disaster, suddenly declared that she desperately needed a quick fag and disappeared outside to get some air. Memories of the accident at the airport in 1985 which killed fifty-five passengers and crew were obviously still uppermost in many peoples' minds at such moments. On that occasion, a plane caught fire on the runway as it was about to take off and all the emergency services had been put on standby that fateful morning just as we were now. Within minutes, the full force of our major accident plan had to be put into action.

With the influx of so many shocked and injured patients arriving all at the same time, it was chaos for a while but the staff coped admirably. The nurses on nights who had been about to go off duty stayed on to assist the day shift, and numerous other members of the nursing and medical staff voluntarily made their way to the hospital to help, even though they were off duty when the news broke. While the actual incident was dealt with rapidly and efficiently, the staff had to deal with many extremely difficult situations, such as passengers who hadn't been able to find their loved ones, or had even been forced to watch helplessly as they perished in the flames and smoke.

It was unbelievably traumatic for everyone involved that day and it took a long time for the memories to fade. Counselling wasn't routinely offered at the time, either to the shocked and injured victims or to those members of the emergency services who had to deal with the aftermath. Many people struggled on for months trying to come to terms with everything they had seen and dealt with; the nursing staff and other services often found it helpful to 'unload' on each other for comfort. Some used black humour as a coping mechanism, others competed as to who could recount their most gruesome experience. One nurse's way of dealing with the pressure was to nip out for a cigarette.

I remember seeing a local television programme discussing the repercussions of the disaster, on which they questioned survivors as to how they had managed to cope in the days and months following the accident. Many of the victims suffered flashbacks and complained that they had not been offered any psychological support. Most now found it a mental challenge to force themselves to get back on to an aeroplane. Some had taken the bull by the horns and had flown straight away and others had attended one of the 'fear of flying' courses put on by their local airport, but for the rest it was likely to be the last time they would ever fly again. As a direct result of this tragic accident it was acknowledged that counselling needed to be offered automatically to everyone involved in any way with major trauma.

My husband and I flew out of Manchester the following day on the same type of Boeing 737 aircraft and I was nearly sick as I boarded the plane. The two cabin crew who were greeting the passengers saw my reluctance to board and asked me how I thought they were feeling, considering that some of their friends and colleagues had died the previous day. If that was supposed to help it failed miserably, as I spent the whole of the flight gripping my seat and praying. My husband on the other hand was quite blasé, his philosophy being that this was probably the safest time to fly as the odds of two such incidents happening so close together would be impossibly high.

Rehearsals for coping with such eventualities take place

regularly and usually involve police, fire, ambulance and casualty staff. The last one I was involved with was a 'pretend' plane crash, similar to the Manchester Airport accident, and ostensibly involved many fatalities and multiple injuries. Young sea and army cadets were our alleged patients and after the 'incident' (following all set protocols as if genuine injuries had occurred) each 'patient' was triaged at the airport by ambulance personnel just as they would be in a real-life emergency. They each had a label attached to their clothing describing the type of injury and whether it was minor, serious, critical or even fatal. Once they had been assessed at the airport, they were then transported to various hospitals in the surrounding areas. Wythenshawe Hospital, being the nearest, would take the first fifty casualties, Withington Hospital the second fifty and so on. When they arrived at the hospital, administration staff were on hand to document each individual, carefully compiling a comprehensive list of admissions. This was, of course, vital because in such a major accident groups easily become separated from each other and may well be taken to different hospitals. Having such a list available also served to assist those anxious families who would be frantically ringing around all the hospitals trying to find out if their loved ones had survived.

Serious and/or critical patients already assessed by ambulance personnel were taken straight into resus or the examination rooms, from where they were rapidly checked and treated before being directed to the appropriate wards or departments. Minor injuries were sent to the waiting area after being booked in and given priority over any other patients already waiting.

For this particular rehearsal I had been stationed in resus along with another staff nurse. Our first patient was a young lad who was brought in by ambulance, trussed up like a sausage roll in several blankets. It was the middle of winter and we were told that all the volunteers had been waiting around for at least two hours for the rehearsal to begin. To make matters worse, there was nowhere for them to take shelter from the biting cold and freezing wind. This little lad was in his sea cadet's uniform, looking every bit the proud junior mariner, grinning from ear to ear and clearly finding the whole exercise very amusing. I looked at the label attached to his chest which clearly stated 'deceased' – I would need a doctor to confirm such a serious condition.

'You're supposed to be dead,' I said with a smile, 'so what are you laughing about?'

He giggled all the more and squirmed around on the stretcher as I tickled him. He had been brought in by ambulance (which was an adventure in itself) that had come screaming through the traffic on blues and twos, and this kid was in his element. By rights, the fact that he was supposed to be dead meant he should have been kept in the ambulance for a doctor to check him over, to make sure that the ambulance men hadn't got it wrong. Then, and only then, he should have been removed to wherever the bodies were being stored. Obviously this part of the rehearsal wasn't followed to the letter, as it would have frightened the volunteers witless to be taken to the mortuary (although I dare say some of the youngsters would probably have enjoyed the trip, but their parents wouldn't have been too pleased). Instead, the young boy was taken to a room designated for the 'deceased' where he received a well-earned drink of juice and a biscuit.

Two more 'victims' quickly followed and, before too long, every room and cubicle in the department was bursting at the seams with pretend patients; some with severe burns, others with multiple trauma injuries, head, arm and leg injuries, some serious cases suffering from smoke inhalation, as well as the dying. It was chaos, but it was organised chaos.

The next 'patient' brought into resus sported a label declaring that he was feeling unwell, had a bad cough, was having difficulty breathing and was in need of immediate attention. An oxygen mask covered his face and he appeared to be genuinely breathless and wheezy. At first I wasn't too sure if he was an actual patient or not because the ambulance crew hadn't passed on any details before they rushed off again. The boy was either a fantastic little actor and deserving of an Oscar or he was genuinely poorly, so I had a chat to him first to try and establish if he was supposed to be a crash victim. He told me that he had been at home in bed for a few days with a bad cough but hadn't wanted to miss the practise at the airport so, after much persuasion, his mum had reluctantly allowed him to take part.

When I checked him out he said that he felt like he was burning up and started to shed a tear or two. At first, I couldn't believe that his mum had let him out of bed in such a state, but I remembered only too well that children can be very persuasive when they want something badly enough. His little face was bright red and he looked terribly despondent; all he wanted now was his mum. The ambulance crews told us that the kids had been raring to go and were all hanging around on the airport apron feeling excited and incredibly self important but that only a few of them had bothered to put on their coats. Not wanting to be thought a wimp or, worse still, sent home, the boy had put on a brave face and said nothing. The cold wind and extended exposure to the elements had exacerbated both his asthma and the virus which he had been fighting for days. He was now feeling very poorly indeed, coughing and wheezing like an old barrel organ. I summoned the doctor immediately and announced that we had a genuine casualty with a bad chest and high temperature. The boy looked totally embarrassed as I made a fuss of him and told the doctor how this enthusiastic young volunteer had left his sick bed to come and help us out with our rehearsal. We both thanked him for his sterling efforts and then, just as the doctor was about to start his examination, his mum walked in. She had been contacted at home by the boy's troop leader, who'd already explained the circumstances to her. Almost immediately after setting foot in the room she launched into the little lad, giving him a good telling off for insisting on going to the airport. She rummaged in her handbag and produced her son's inhaler (which he was supposed to have kept in his pocket, but had forgotten and left on the kitchen table) and couldn't stop apologising to the doctor for causing us so much trouble.

I was tempted to speak up for the child, but if he had been my son I would have probably done exactly the same, so I kept quiet and said nothing. The doctor examined him carefully, particularly his wheezy chest, before deciding that the boy should first try using his inhaler to see if there was any improvement. If that didn't work, he would have to be given a nebuliser (a device used to administer liquid medication in the form of a mist which is inhaled into the lungs via a special oxygen mask). He quickly began to recover, though, and was moved into cas obs as soon as his breathing had stabilised, before eventually being sent home with antibiotics and a bottle of Calpol to bring down his temperature. Now that he had his mum with him and was feeling much better he seemed thrilled to bits with all the attention he had received and went home beaming with pleasure. I'm sure that he had a good story to tell when he next saw his friends again.

The rest of the rehearsal went well. Having 'pretend' patients with 'pretend' injuries may not equate to dealing with the real thing, and the pressure and urgency of a real emergency may be missing, but these rehearsals enable each emergency service to carry out a critical analysis of their performance and revise their own protocols where necessary.

Throughout the rehearsals, genuine emergencies were still being brought in, which tended to complicate matters but this would, of course, be the case in a real-life situation, too. Regardless of numbers, all you can ever do is prioritise the most seriously injured patients and deal with them first.

Chapter 13

12.00am

Jeanne soon gave us the good news that the all-clear had been issued from the airport and we all breathed just a little easier. The whole world accompanied by several of their sozzled acquaintances seemed to descend on Wythenshawe Hospital as the pubs started turning them out, and midnight came and went without any of us even noticing. We had heard a garbled, drunken rendition of Auld Lang Syne coming from the waiting room at one point, but we were far too busy to care. Most of the patients had been drinking heavily and had fallen over or been punched, and the suture room was a conveyer belt of lacerations waiting to be stitched up. The waiting room was full to capacity with many more overflowing into the corridors, where they were quietly snoozing on the hard floors or moaning at the top of their voices about having to wait.

The influx of minor injuries and stretcher patients had

gradually built up and every nurse was now fully occupied, hurrying around between the different areas calling patients in, taking those who were being admitted up to the wards, cleaning wounds and putting in stitches. I was assisting Dr Cross, who was concentrating on trying to extract two quite different foreign objects from the bodily orifices into which they had been inappropriately inserted. The first from a child who had been experimenting to see just how far up his nose he could push a small bead, and the other from a gentleman who quite frankly ought to have known better where NOT to hide things; although the less said about the object and which particular orifice the better. Throughout all this activity the outside telephone line seemed to ring non-stop, and each time whoever was nearest had to stop what they were doing to go and answer it.

One such call was picked up by Jeanne who just happened to be passing at that moment. In general these calls were mainly from people enquiring about a friend or relative, or asking how long they were likely to be kept waiting if they came in with an injury, but on this occasion Jeanne's face registered her annoyance as she listened to the person on the line. All we heard was a very tetchy, 'No I'm sorry, she's not on duty tonight,' before she literally slammed the phone down. She immediately used an internal line to ring the switchboard and say, 'If that caller rings back please don't put him through to Casualty again. I have better things to do than to deal with idiots.'

We all looked at each other, puzzled. There had been no explanation given to the lady on switch, presumably because Jeanne didn't want patients nearby to hear what had been said to her, but she was looking unusually rattled as she disappeared off into resus to deal with a patient who had just been brought in by emergency ambulance.

The first quiet moment we had, one of the girls asked her about the call and Jeanne was still fuming. When she picked up the receiver she heard giggling from what clearly sounded like a group of teenagers, before the caller rudely inquired, 'Are you the nurse with the big tits?'

Initially, we all had a good laugh – not at the moron on the telephone, but at Jeanne's quick-witted reply. Strangely, I had never seen her so flustered by anything in all the years she had worked at Wythenshawe and, personally, I felt quite indignant that someone could be so immature and irresponsible. We could have been literally in the middle of a life or death situation. I wonder what the caller would have thought if a nurse or doctor had disrupted the urgent and essential care of someone they loved in order to answer such a call. Despite having previously worked in two other busy Casualty departments, I can honestly say that I had never before experienced this level of mindless ignorance.

Soon afterwards, one of the patients from the minor injuries area arrived back from X-ray carrying a large brown envelope containing a number of films of both her wrists. It is always quite amusing watching patients as they come back from X-ray, because they invariably take a peek without the least idea of what they are looking at. Despite her injuries she had managed to take one of the films out of its envelope to have a quick nosey, and was awkwardly turning it this way and that, trying to work out which was the right way round. Even nurses have problems sometimes, so she had no chance.

Elsie was an elderly lady who had fallen on black ice earlier that evening while carrying her shopping from the supermarket. Without any warning, she completely lost her footing, sending the bags of shopping skywards and herself towards the ground, her hands outstretched to break her fall. When her husband brought Elsie into Casualty, she was quite badly shaken up and in a great deal of pain. The doctor examined her, requested that both her arms be put in slings, and sent her straight to X-ray. He was in no doubt that at least one of her wrists was broken, with the strong possibility of them both having suffered the same fate. He could tell just by looking at the shape of her right wrist, that she had sustained a Colles' fracture – the radius had been fractured and displaced in the fall, thus giving the hand an unmistakeable shape like the back of a fork. Sometimes the second bone, the ulna, is also fractured but, either way, it meant that she was likely to be given a light anaesthetic to pull the deformed arm straight, at the very least, before a plaster was applied.

The Colles' fracture is very commonly seen in older people, particularly women who may have osteoporosis (a weakening of the bones due to a lack of calcium as they get older – also known as brittle bones) and is usually sustained by a person falling forward on to a hard surface and breaking their fall with extended outstretched hands, which was exactly what this lady had done. Depending on how bad the fracture is, this type of break can be treated in three ways. The first, and easiest to deal with, is if the fracture is undisplaced, that is to say the ends of the broken bone are in alignment, which usually requires nothing more than a simple plaster of Paris. The second method occurs when it is a slightly more complicated fracture because the bones are out of alignment (displaced). In this case, the fracture is manipulated back into place, usually requiring a light general anaesthetic, before plaster of Paris is applied. The third type of treatment required is for a compound fracture. This is a far more complicated injury, where the bones have actually snapped and pushed through the tissues. In such a case, the patient would be admitted to the ortho-paedic ward for an urgent operation to manipulate the bones into position and, depending on the severity of the damage, stabilise and fix the bones with a series of screws, pins and plates.

Putting the films up on the illuminated screen in the doctors' office allowed him to confirm the diagnosis that Elsie had, in fact, managed to break both her wrists; the right arm required a manipulation of the bones while under a light general anaesthetic (followed by a plaster), while the left only required a straightforward plaster of Paris.

What a way to see in the new year for this poor woman. She was quite stoical about the proposed treatments when the doctor first gave her this news and, in fact, seemed quite enthused at the prospect of her husband having to carry out all the household chores for a change, including the cooking and ironing. However, the pleased expression on her face began to fade pretty rapidly when some practical individual smilingly pointed out: 'Yes, but just wait until you want to take a bath or your hair needs washing. Or, even worse, when you need to go to the toilet! Then what will you do?'

She had obviously not even contemplated such everyday scenarios and her initial good humour continued to ebb away rapidly as the realities of her situation began to sink in. Her husband's face wasn't exactly a picture of undiluted happiness either.

I was quite surprised to find that at Wythenshawe, unlike Blackburn and Blackpool, the casualty doctors were responsible for carrying out the simple MUAs (manipulation under anaesthetic) in the department themselves, rather than referring them to the orthopaedic doctors who dealt with them from the wards.

The anaesthetist on call would be summoned and then, after going through the usual safety checks to make sure the patient was fit for anaesthetic (i.e. enquiring when they last had anything to eat and drink; what [if any] medications they were taking; had they had an anaesthetic before; did they have any allergies etc.), they would be taken into the plaster theatre in Casualty and given a light general anaesthetic before undergoing the procedure. Each one of these enquiries can be vitally important. If the patient has recently eaten or drunk anything (i.e. within the last six hours), then they may vomit and choke to death under anaesthetic. If they are taking medications, these can cause adverse reactions and need to be documented, and known allergies should be noted because this information can affect the medication prescribed during or after anaesthetic.

Fortunately, apart from a cup of tea and one slice of toast, this lady hadn't eaten or drunk anything since lunchtime, and in general was fit and well for her age. After explaining the procedure to her, she was asked to sign a consent form (which she obviously couldn't very well complete for herself, so her husband signed on her behalf) and was then moved into casualty theatre. Once there I dealt first with the undisplaced fracture by applying a back slab to it. This is a half plaster that is placed on the back of an injured limb and then secured with a bandage, to allow for any potential swelling, and left on for between twelve and twenty-four hours. After this, it is checked again before the full plaster is applied. We then waited for the anaesthetist and the casualty doctor to complete the appropriate paperwork before she was given an anaesthetic to treat her more severely damaged right arm.

Despite receiving and benefitting from what I still regard as the best type of training possible as a student nurse, when I started at Wythenshawe I had never actually assisted a doctor with an MUA. The hospital insisted that before being allowed to carry out a new procedure, whether you were qualified or not, you had to undergo supervised training until you felt and were deemed competent. I had watched many manipulations being carried out, but the very first time I assisted myself it made me grit my teeth. I was advised that there was nothing to it, but I wasn't too sure when I saw the two doctors and supervising sister glance at each other and exchange a sly grin. The patient was laid down reasonably flat and the anaesthetist administered his knock-out potion. Once he was confident that the patient was sound asleep, he nodded to the casualty doctor in charge of the procedure to go ahead. Like my present patient, that first patient had also fallen and fractured her wrist. The doctor held the x-ray up to the light to show me how displaced the bones were, and told me that our job was to pull on the arm as hard as we could, with me gripping the upper part of the radius near to the elbow and pulling towards me, while he at the same time pulled in the opposite direction, twisting, bending and tugging the bones until they were in perfect alignment. It was only then, when the bones were in place, that a back slab could be applied.

It may sound pretty straightforward but, in reality, the bones don't always go back in place without a struggle, and you end up doing a tug of war with the poor individual's arm being used as the rope. It certainly explained to me why some people experienced varying levels of discomfort afterwards.

Hearing and feeling the ends of the broken bones grating together as the doctor tried to get the fractures aligned made me squirm that first time but, after a few, I got used to the experience and came to find the whole thing quite satisfying, especially when the bones went back into place easily and there was no sign of any deformity (which can easily happen if the bones are badly broken). Since that first occasion I had assisted in literally dozens of manipulations and become quite proficient, although I still cringe when the grinding gets a little too loud.

All went well this time and, before too long, Elsie was sitting up in cas obs with both arms encased in plaster and supported by slings; although, now she was looking a little sorry for herself.

For very different reasons this incident also reminded me of an elderly man I had dealt with two or three weeks previously. Being stubborn (or stoical, depending on how you see it), and in spite of the icy pavements, he still insisted on doing his own shopping but he wasn't very steady on his feet, even under normal circumstances. On his way back from the corner shop, he had managed to reach his front door without any problem when, just as he was about to open it, he went down and landed awkwardly on his wrist. A neighbour came to his assistance and rang for an ambulance, before contacting his daughter who arrived at the hospital shortly after her father. X-rays showed that he, too, had sustained a Colles' fracture that necessitated him having a light general anaesthetic to straighten the bones, followed by the usual back slab and sling to elevate the arm. His recovery from the anaesthetic was swift and uneventful so, as soon as the doctors felt he was fit for discharge, I went to ask him about his home situation.

It is always hospital policy that if a patient is elderly and lives alone they are either encouraged to stay in hospital overnight so they can be seen the following morning for a plaster check, or alternatively a relative is asked to keep an eye on them to make sure that they are coping with the added encumbrance of a cast and sling until they can return for the check.

Swelling can occur after any injury, especially if it has been pummelled and pulled about during manipulation, and if there is a plaster cast restricting the area the patient's circulation can become impeded (with obvious serious consequences). All patients with plaster casts, regardless which limb is affected, are usually given written instructions advising them what to do if their fingers or toes turn blue, white or black and feel icy cold, dead or increasingly painful. These symptoms always require prompt attention and are treated as an emergency – the plaster is either removed or split open to relieve the pressure or restriction.

I dutifully asked the elderly gent if he would stay in overnight, but he looked horrified at the thought and refused outright even to consider doing so. Before he could say another word, his daughter interrupted the conversation and assured me that she would make sure he was looked after and promised to bring him back in the morning for a plaster check, or even earlier if necessary. As luck would have it, I documented this conversation on his casualty card and took a note of the daughter's details, because the following day his son (who immediately went to great pains to tell us that he was a solicitor, presumably because it was supposed to impress or intimidate us), rang the hospital to put in a complaint that someone had sent his frail old father home alone to fend for himself after having been given an anaesthetic, and he was now having to struggle about with his arm in a sling. I was absolutely livid and desperately wanted to ring this man and refute his complaint, but regrettably wasn't allowed to do so. I fully appreciate that the hospital want or need to standardise their response to all complaints for legal reasons, but I found it infuriating and supremely frustrating that staff aren't given the opportunity to defend themselves, because I would never dream of treating an elderly person with disregard or disrespect and it was hurtful that people should think otherwise.

Elsie, on the other hand, had decided to stay in overnight – I suspect her husband wanted one last night of peace before he was on call all day, every day until her recovery! I dare say that over the next few weeks she would certainly discover who her real friends were.

Chapter 14

12.45am

Ever since the night staff had come on duty, we had been kept constantly on the go; as soon as we finished dealing with one case another was inevitably waiting. At one point, Wendy and I had been clearing out one of the examination rooms after a patient had been discharged and we were returning the stretcher to the bay near the rear doors, when we saw an ambulance on its way. The blue emergency lights weren't flashing but we could see several figures inside, so we decided to go out to the ambulance bay to give the occupants a warm Wythenshawe welcome.

As it pulled up and backed into the bay, the ambulance doors were flung open by the crew and we could see two young, white males in their mid- to late twenties looking very sorry for themselves. They were experiencing some difficulty in getting to their feet and the ambulance men told us that the two lads had been involved in a road traffic accident on their motor bikes, along with about six of their friends who were following along behind. These two were thankfully the only ones who had been hurt but they appeared to be in a great deal of pain, although the crew said their injuries were mainly superficial.

Wendy was on fine form; as these two unfortunate individuals gingerly inched their way down the ambulance steps, she stood there with a huge grin on her face, hands on hips like a triumphant traffic warden. Introduced to us as Brian and James, we did a double take when we saw their rather unconventional appearance; both were sporting really long, black dreadlocks, a procession of studs and rings in each ear, a handful of multicoloured nostril accessories and were wearing floor-length, RAF surplus, blue trench coats and knee-length, heavy, leather boots. After setting foot back on terra firma, they looked shocked and distinctly apprehensive.

The pair appeared even more worried when Wendy breezed forward, stood in front of them and said to Brian, 'Right, lad, you're mine.'

When she grabbed hold of his arm and linked it firmly into hers, he seemed panic-stricken and turned around to his mate in desperation, looking for support.

Seeing the naked fear on his face, she grinned and said reassuringly, 'Come on, chuck, you'll be all right. Come with your Auntie Wendy; I'll look after you.' Before leading him away, she turned pityingly to James and, pointing towards me, declared, 'Sorry, lad, you've drawn the short straw; you're stuck with Timberdick.'

Everybody laughed, including the two ambulance men, and with perfect timing their next call of duty sounded on the radio, so they quickly briefed us about the accident and the subsequent injuries our two brave little soldiers had sustained, before disappearing off down the road, blue lights flashing.

Apparently the two lads had been riding their motorbikes on a minor country road with their friends trying to find the address of a proposed party, when they went round a sharp bend and hit a patch of black ice. A split second later they found themselves sliding helplessly down the road on their backsides as their momentum carried them along. They were not wearing protective leather trousers, so they had both sustained rather nasty friction burns that were not only grazed and bleeding but also 'pebble-dashed' with frozen cow poo, dried mud, gravel and everything else that just happened to be lying around in the road at the time.

From the next cubicle, I could hear Wendy oohing and aahing at the sight of the lacerated skin and filthy grazes on Brian's bottom, followed by the moan of pain as she tried carefully to peel off his bloodied trousers. Likewise, my boy James was in a similar predicament. Looking at the damage, Wendy and I both agreed afterwards that the two lads were extremely fortunate to have avoided much more serious injuries. As I started to remove James's trousers, his posterior looked like it had been attacked with a cheese grater and large areas of skin on both buttocks and the tops of his thighs were deeply scuffed and ingrained with filth. It looked like a piece of raw meat that had been dragged along behind a car. Heaven only knows what it must have felt like but, if I was any sort of judge, he was not going to be able to sit down comfortably any time soon and the injuries were going to take many weeks to heal.

Dr Cross had been kept busy ever since his arrival on duty. He had already got through quite a number of patients but, even though we had not received the lad's cards yet, he came straight over to check on our two bikers and flinched when he saw what a mess they were in. After carefully examining each of them for further injuries, he stood for a moment, deliberating how best to tackle their shredded flesh. In the end, he decided that it would be less uncomfortable for them to have local anaesthetic gel smeared over the whole wound (which unfortunately, even on a small cut, stings like hell), since he felt that this was preferable to them having to endure numerous injections of local anaesthetic in and around every part of the damaged area. I'm not sure that in their position I would have welcomed either of these options, but there was no viable alternative, because administering a general anaesthetic carries far too great a risk for what are really only superficial injuries, and was therefore not an option in these circumstances. Both were prescribed a tetanus booster and an antibiotic injection, to be followed by a full course of antibiotic tablets to prevent infection. The two lads were groaning in anticipation of the injections, which really amused me, considering all their body piercings, as they'd probably not given the needles a second thought when having those done. It was nearly always the big, tough-looking, mouthy characters who wimped out when it came to needles, and I can recall many who have turned white with fear and passed out at the mere sight of a nurse heading in their direction with a hypodermic in hand.

Frightening people with needles was a popular trick to play on rookie police officers who had perhaps suffered a minor injury in the line of duty, but had never been to Wythenshawe Hospital before or encountered one of the 'psycho' nurses on Casualty. He/she would usually turn up after having been sent in by their duty sergeant to get their injury checked out, and we would have been pre-warned of their arrival. The doctor would examine their injury first, as normal, before prescribing whatever treatment was required. If something like an anti-tetanus or antibiotic injection was required then, without discussing it with the patient, the chosen sadist would clean the wound ever so gently, smiling and reassuring them that they were indeed likely to survive into old age, before producing the biggest needle and syringe that could be found in the department, which had been filled in advance with bright red Mercurochrome antiseptic for effect. We'd then sit back to watch their reaction, and it was usually a very gratifying experience!

During one such initiation, I remember a young male officer turning completely ashen and almost fainting, before jumping up from the chair and telling the nurse to 'Sod off!' A few of us who had been watching in the wings smiled in anticipation as our colleague kept a straight face and insisted that he vitally needed this injection, telling him sternly to drop his pants or she would ring his sergeant. He tentatively unfastened his trousers and leant over the couch, his face now distinctly green and taut in anticipation of the agony to come. Behind his back the nurse picked up the correct syringe (which was in fact the smallest we use in the department) and put it swiftly into his buttock without him so much as flinching. As she walked away, the officer straightened up and looked around in surprise at having felt so little discomfort, then saw her standing there with a big smile on her face brandishing both syringes, the larger of the two still brimming with vivid red antiseptic. The episode provided a bit of light relief at the time and the young officer was a good sport about it, but he warned us to make sure our tax discs were up to date!

Obviously, we weren't going to play such a trick on our two bikers – they had an uncomfortable enough time in prospect as it was. After first warning them that the gel was going to sting a little, Wendy and I applied the anaesthetic as quickly and as gently as possible to their raw bits before making a rapid retreat to give it time to absorb (and also to shelter our delicate ears from the eruption of bad language that inevitably followed). Their vocabulary was triple-x-rated stuff but, in all fairness, no one could blame them.

We left the two alone for a few minutes to contemplate their fate while the anaesthetic took effect and went across to have a quick word with Jenny on reception. She was looking dog-tired from the previous night, which she said had been even busier than expected but, like us, she was still hoping, although not exactly optimistic, that the patients would not be quite as demanding tonight. She handed over the lads' casualty cards, which had been filled in by their friends who had turned up having followed the ambulance to the hospital, and mentioned that she had seen a very similar case come in when she was on duty only two or three months before, where a female pillion passenger had been thrown at speed over the handlebars of her boyfriend's motorbike. The young woman, like this pair, had been wearing ordinary jeans. After being projected along the road at speed on her buttocks, she needed to be admitted to hospital with very serious injuries that required major surgery. Extensive damage was caused not only to her bottom but even to her pelvic organs and, after being in hospital for several weeks, she was left with permanent damage. Strong leather trousers could possibly have given her greater protection and may well have reduced the severity of the damage, but no protective clothing will completely protect a biker in such an horrific accident.

After about five minutes, Wendy and I went back to

check on Brian and James to see if the anaesthetic had worked, and we had to smile at the sight of the two of them lying face down on the stretchers with their bare bums stuck up in the air waiting for our tender ministrations. The gel had done its job well and their nether regions were now suitably numb, so for the next half hour or so we sat and literally scrubbed all the dirt and gravel out of their skin, using a sterile nail brush and hydrogen peroxide, removing the bigger pieces of gravel with sterile forceps. It was a painstaking and bloody task, but was actually quite satisfying in a way and, thankfully, they couldn't feel a thing. Wendy was still trying to make Brian laugh by suggesting she might have the front of her house pebble-dashed with the gravel she had picked out of his rear end, while I was quietly concentrating on removing a rather large piece of stone embedded quite deep in James's gluteus maximus, which I couldn't see but could definitely feel. Using a pair of fine sterile tweezers and squeezing a little more anaesthetic gel into the wound, I managed to obtain a grip on the object several times but, for some reason, it stubbornly refused to budge. Putting even more anaesthetic gel on to the area, I tried again and this time I got a really firm grip. I pulled as hard as I could and out popped a triangular piece of gravel that appeared to be twice the size of the hole from which it had just emerged. As I sat back smugly to admire my handiwork, I taunted Wendy that mine was much bigger and better than hers.

'No chance,' she retorted, laughing as she dropped another lump of tarmac into a kidney bowl where her own rockery was growing steadily.

Once we were both fully satisfied that all the gravel and dirt had been removed, we cleaned the wounds thoroughly for the final time, applied an antiseptic dressing covered by thick sterile padding (to help cushion the injuries) and went to get Dr Cross to write up their casualty cards before sorting out their injections.

Triplopen was the penicillin injection of choice at that time and was always given for particularly dirty wounds. A very thick white liquid administered to the upper outer quadrant of the buttock, it was almost guaranteed to hurt like the devil but was brilliant for keeping infections at bay. I gave James his tetanus injection first, knowing that at least that wouldn't hurt as much as the Triplopen, but when I pre-warned him that the second injection had to go into his bottom and might hurt just a teeny weeny bit, I felt him tense up in anticipation. As the needle went in and the creamy liquid was pushed home, he bit on to his hand and swore like a trooper, groaning loudly with the pain. I totally sympathised with him because I knew exactly how it felt, having twice been on the receiving end myself.

As I was chatting to James about the wound management for his injuries, there was an almighty yell from the adjoining cubicle as Wendy jabbed Brian with the magic liquid. Brian started cursing her and Wendy was telling him not to be such a wimp, both of them laughing their heads off. The banter between them was flowing thick and fast, and it was clear that the two had struck up quite a rapport in such a short time.

Before our road surfers departed, they were each given a course of antibiotics to take home and then thanked us for looking after them. They shook our hands and slowly but painfully hobbled out of the department. The tattered remnants of their blood-stained Levis hung dejectedly down around their knees in threads, and they were probably feeling the discomfort of the penicillin injection more than their initial injuries, not yet realising that they would feel a lot worse when the anaesthetic gel wore off. A sudden roar went up from the waiting room where several of their friends were still waiting for them and promises were made to take them for a pint or two on the way home.

'No alcohol allowed on penicillin,' Wendy and I shouted in unison, but from the looks we received I don't think they intended to take too much notice. Despite their slightly intimidating appearance, the pair of them had been two of the most pleasant, polite young men either of us had come across for some considerable time.

After the gang of bikers had left the building I couldn't wait to take a closer look at Dr Cross. I had noticed a rather nasty discolouration under his eye and white sticky tape holding the bridge of his spectacles together but obviously wasn't going to question him in front of the patients. I was dying to know what had happened. When I eventually cornered him for a moment, although he was clearly fed up by now with repeating the story, he told me that, on the previous night, the middle-aged son of a female patient had taken offence when asked politely to leave the examination room while his mother was being examined. The doctor was only attempting to be sensitive to the old lady and allowing her to retain some dignity but the man was inebriated, swaying around, stumbling into equipment and generally being a pain in the backside. For some reason he became belligerent and refused to leave and, when Dr Cross insisted, the man punched him twice in the face; the first time, breaking his glasses, the second punch knocking him to the floor. The perpetrator was dragged out of the examination room by two of the porters who heard the fracas and he was ejected from the hospital until he had calmed down. Because the drunk's mum was seriously ill, Dr Cross very charitably made allowances for him and promised not to involve the police, provided the man behaved himself. He was warned in no uncertain terms that if he so much as opened his mouth again or became obstructive in any way, then the doctor would bring charges against him for common assault. The message seemed to filter through the booze this time and, although no apology was forthcoming, his behaviour was much improved from then on. (No doubt the shock of being manhandled and thrown out into the cold had brought him back to his senses and perhaps sobered him up a little.)

Not having yet had the opportunity to purchase any replacement glasses, Dr Cross was walking around Casualty looking like Jack Duckworth from *Coronation Street*. Tall and a little overweight, slightly unkempt (he famously only ever ironed the front of his shirts) and with hair that always looked like it needed a cut, he was definitely the Worzel Gummidge of the department. Unmarried, the nurses in Casualty felt that he needed a good woman to smarten him up and we knew that Helen fancied him. Whatever his appearance, he was a quick, confident clinician with a pleasant demeanour and I always found him a pleasure to work with. The fact that he hadn't brought charges against this man was typical of his generosity; many would have thrown the book at him.

When trouble occurs in Casualty, it can be quite alarming for patients and staff alike. We were lucky and grateful to have such a good group of porters on nights, as one or two of them would always come to our assistance if a situation seemed to be getting out of control. Barry, one of our porters with many years' experience, was the person we tended to rely on far more frequently than we probably had any right to. After all, he wasn't paid to be our bodyguard but he seemed to have the knack of always being there at the right time, and tonight was one of those occasions.

A drunk had made his own way into the department, purportedly after falling on some ice, and had sustained a small but quite deep cut to the back of his head. According to his version of events, the cut was caused by glass from a broken bottle that just happened to be lying around in the pub car park, but from his appearance he looked to us like he had been in a fight. His face was discoloured and scratched and his bottom lip was swelling up by the minute. On arrival into Casualty, the man and a friend who had come with him immediately began shouting the odds when Jenny informed them that the waiting time was likely to be at least two hours or more. She commendably maintained a professional attitude and apologised but said that unfortunately there was nothing she could do about it. This man had obviously seen the long queue of people waiting and decided that he needed to be seen as a priority. Jenny patiently pointed out all the other patients to him, quite a few of them nursing blood-soaked bandages on their injuries, too, and said she would get a nurse to cover his wound with a dressing. She asked him politely to sit down and wait until someone could come out to take a look. Kath wasn't in the middle of anything so she got the dubious pleasure. She went out to check the gash on his head and explained that she wasn't able to do anything other than cover up the cut until he had been seen by the doctor, at which point he started ranting on about the bloody NHS and the effing useless uncaring staff. His language became so totally outrageous that Kath informed Jeanne, who came out to see what was going on. Other patients who had been sitting waiting patiently started to grumble, several telling him forcefully to shut up and sit down. Before too long, the situation had deteriorated even further when one or two of them threatened to punch his lights out if he didn't behave, warning him in no uncertain terms that there was no way he was going to be treated before them. Jeanne's presence and her explanation as to why he had to wait like everyone else made not a jot of difference to his behaviour so, after warning the stroppy individual several more times to watch his language and keep his voice down, she eventually decided to call the police.

Ken and James arrived for the second time that night and quickly warned the man that he would be arrested if he didn't quieten down. Unbelievably, the drunk took a swing at one of them and the next moment all three were struggling on the floor as the officers tried to put handcuffs on him. Although he wasn't a big bloke, he appeared to be getting the upper hand and was dishing out several heavy punches. Enter Barry, who was not exactly a tall man either but kept himself extremely fit doing martial arts; his physique was outstanding for his forty-odd years of age and comprised about ninety-nine per cent muscle. He just happened to be returning to Casualty with Chris, after taking a patient up to the ward, when he came across this little mêlée. Without hesitation, he pitched in to help the officers and, much to everyone's satisfaction, within seconds had the lad in a ju-jitsu hold that had him begging for mercy. His friend had sensibly kept well away from the fisticuffs and was desperately urging his mate to calm down. Barry had a grip on the lad's thumb which put such excruciating pressure on the joint that the slightest movement was agony. Every time the drunk tried to move, Barry simply squeezed a little harder to sustain the pressure and had such complete control that the two officers were able to relinquish their own grip entirely. Barry had barely broken into a sweat and several people started applauding to show their respect, when he stood up with an embarrassed grin on his face and frog-marched the drunk out of the waiting room.

Much to everyone's disgust, the patient did in fact get his own way in the end, because the police officers thought it wise to remove him from the department as quickly as possible. After checking him over, Dr Cross asked Kath to stitch up his cut before he was promptly handed over to the officers to start the new year in a police cell. The other patients saw the drunk being taken out in handcuffs and put into a van, so nobody really complained too much, although one individual took umbrage and started whingeing loudly that staff had allowed the man to jump the queue. Wendy had a go at him and asked him what he suggested we should have done. Without waiting for a reply, she walked away in disgust, while several voices in the waiting room echoed their frustration and chimed in to tell the man to shut his mouth.

★

Having seen how busy we were earlier in the evening, Big Daft Denis and Peter decided to call back and check in on us to make sure that all was well. Up to this point, the numbers of patients waiting had fluctuated between steady and busy; pretty much similar to a regular Saturday night but, now that we had seen the back of this one idiot, it was at least a bit quieter. Looking very official, the dynamic duo quietly circulated around the department making their presence apparent to the waiting hordes, chatting amiably to them and sympathising with them for having to wait so long. Denis at one point had his trouser leg rolled up to the knee to show a patient his own bandaged leg, which I seem to remember he had injured during a game of rugby. He was no doubt hoping for a bit of sympathy but really he wanted to get them all laughing and they were soon comparing their own ailments and injuries like a bunch of kids in the school playground.

After they had milked their captive audience in the waiting room, the two officers popped into the treatment area. Denis smiled at several patients as they quietly nodded off in their cubicles waiting to be seen and offered to stitch them up himself. In return, he received several exotic suggestions that I honestly didn't understand! He waved airily at Jeanne as she breathlessly dashed in and out of the resus room without a second to stop and chat, while I was busy on my hands and knees strapping up a lady's sprained ankle. Chris and Theresa were in the suture room trying to persuade a little boy (who needed to have stitches put in his knee) that he wouldn't feel a thing because he had been given local anaesthetic. Wendy had disappeared into the plaster room to put a cast on a man's foot who had fallen down a flight of stairs, Cynthia was settled for the night in cas obs, which was now full to capacity with patients who were staying overnight (which probably meant she'd have a nice quiet night) and Anita was tidying up in resus after Jeanne had been in there dealing with an asthmatic.

After surveying all the activity, Denis and Peter disappeared without saying a word, only to return about ten minutes later with a large tray of teas and a plate of biscuits. Before they could sit down to enjoy a break, they had to leave it and run, after being summoned urgently on their radios, but it certainly put a welcome smile back on our faces. One cheeky mare (who shall remain nameless, only because I don't like admitting it was me) shouted after them, 'Bring us some chocolate next time you're passing!'

Shortly afterwards, I was on my hands and knees yet again as I treated a man who had dropped something particularly heavy on his big toe. Blood was trapped under the nail and, unable to escape, it was causing him excruciating pain. The only way to treat this injury was to make a hole in the nail in order to release the blood, which in turn relieved the build up of pressure. Dr Cross asked me to trephine the patient's nail, which involved putting a hot needle through the nail, so I was totally consumed with what I was doing and was so busy that I ignored the loud theatrical, 'Pssssssst!' coming from somewhere behind me. The second time it happened, I thought it was simply someone messing about, so again took no notice. Finally, a frustrated voice boomed, 'You didn't ignore me in bed last night, woman, did you?'

A collective snigger went up from the row of cubicles as I turned around to see Denis standing there, grinning from ear to ear and beckoning me into the doctors' office. I finished putting a dressing on the patient's toe and sent him home, before quickly tidying the cubicle and going into the office to see what could be so important. I felt my face start to flush with embarrassment as I knew that several patients were straining their ears to find out what was going to happen next. As I went into the room, Denis dramatically turned his tunic pockets out on to the desk – they were stuffed with at least a dozen chocolate bars. The girls were all pleased to bits, since it didn't look like we would be getting much of an opportunity to eat our party food any time soon. Usually, even on the busiest shifts, we manage to grab a few minutes break at regular intervals, but tonight it didn't look like it was going to work out that way. This carbohydrate treat (I suppose, you could argue they were medicinal) would at least keep us going for a while.

Denis and Peter were both very popular with all the nurses; their wicked sense of humour and their thoughtfulness meant a great deal to us. Denis was the comedian; Peter was quieter but also liked a laugh and a joke. One afternoon, I had just come out of M&S in nearby Altrincham town centre laden with four heavy shopping bags, when out of the blue I was grabbed from behind and lifted bodily into the air. There was Denis with a big, stupid grin on his face, cradling me and my shopping in his arms like a baby and totally ignoring all my pleas to put me down. I was very conscious that I must have been flashing my knickers to half the town's population and struggled desperately in an effort to escape his clutches. I had no chance; he wasn't even breaking sweat. A large number of shoppers and office workers on their lunch breaks stopped to watch the floor show, laughing as he carried me half way down the precinct, smiling and waving at many of the shop assistants in the large stores as we went along. I could have killed him, but settled for thumping him as hard as I could, which made no impression on him whatsoever. He eventually set me back down on my feet and waved me on my way, promising to call in to Casualty again soon, where he expected a hot cuppa as reward for helping me to carry my shopping. He didn't give two hoots about anything. Provided he put a smile on people's faces while enjoying his job, he seemed to be perfectly happy. His wife and children must have wondered what was coming next with that crazy man.

Chapter 15

1.30am

Jeanne decided that we should all take short breaks in pairs, because otherwise we weren't going to get anything to eat at all. Wendy and Chris went first, while the rest of us spread ourselves out and carried on, prioritising the patients as we went along. Jeanne went off into the suture room to see if she could clear a backlog of patients who had already been seen by the doctor but were now just sitting around awaiting their stitches. Kath and Theresa were dealing with the stretcher cases, and I carried on with treatments on the minor injuries side, while Anita took some food down to Cynthia.

As I was tidying up the end cubicle, after sorting out the last patient in that group, I couldn't help but notice a rough-looking, middle-aged man prowling around the treatment area muttering incoherently under his breath, his face twisted in a dark, malevolent expression. He was carrying what appeared to be a rolled up wet towel in his right hand, which he was systematically slapping threateningly into the palm of his left hand with considerable force. I am not easily frightened and have dealt with any number of tough and potentially violent characters in my career, but this man sent shivers down my spine. His body language screamed out to me that I needed to be cautious, so I decided to keep a close eye on him for a few minutes to see what he was up to. He reminded me of a caged animal wandering aimlessly backwards and forwards, fierce and angry and ready to lash out. He never once made eye contact or spoke to any member of staff (or anyone else for that matter) either to say who he was or what he was doing there. I quickly went around the other nurses to ask if they knew anything about him, but no one had a clue, so I went to find Jeanne because I had a sense of foreboding that this man spelled trouble.

Jeanne was still busy in the suture room dealing with a lady who was in a terrible state. Covered in blood, she had numerous abrasions all over her face; both eyes were virtually closed due to bruising and swelling, and her nose and mouth were split open and bleeding freely. The middle-aged woman was shaking and sobbing uncontrollably. At this point, just as Jeanne was about to clean the patient up, I interrupted and asked if I could have a quick word with her outside. I didn't want to alarm the patient, who looked like she had more than enough on her plate already, but I felt that Jeanne needed to be alerted to this man's presence immediately. I pointed him out and, although she had never met him before, from the description she had been given by the ambulance crew Jeanne was fairly sure he was her patient's husband. This lady had apparently insisted to the ambulance crew that she had fallen down the stairs but, to their experienced eyes, her injuries were not consistent with a fall and, besides which, she looked absolutely terrified. The ambulance men told Jeanne that the lady's husband was adamant he was coming to the hospital, insisting that he wanted to be with his wife. Seeing his aggressive demeanour and her terror, they had no intention of allowing him to ride in the back of the ambulance, so had advised him to follow them by car in case his wife was discharged later and needed him to take her home. This had been the only way they could keep the two apart. They had, of course, seen it all many times before and were convinced that this was a case of domestic violence; it certainly didn't take a genius to work it out and, presumably, he was now hanging around to make sure she didn't tell anyone what really happened.

Dr Cross examined the lady and was also convinced that she had been punched in the face several times yet, for some reason, she was still reluctant to admit the truth. He put a few stitches in her nose and lip but, until the patient acknowledged what really happened, there was nothing more he could do, other than to leave her in Jeanne's capable hands.

Over the years various neighbours had called the police many times after hearing screams coming from the house, but every time the police went to investigate, his wife was always too afraid to speak out and refused to bring charges against the man. On numerous occasions she had even made excuses for him, saying that she loved him and didn't want him to be locked up, that it was probably all her own fault for upsetting him. And so the abuse had continued, she once confiding to a close neighbour that he only ever struck her where the bruises wouldn't show. He had never previously hit her in the face, nor had he caused an injury which warranted her having to come to hospital, yet this time he appeared to have gone completely over the top. After being in the pub all day, he had come home stinking drunk on this occasion and had set about her when his supper wasn't ready on the table for him. Using her as a punch bag, he had struck her about the head several times before knocking her to the floor and kicking her around the room. Now, at long last, the lady finally decided that he'd gone too far and plucked up the courage to do something about it. She told Jeanne that this time she definitely intended to have him charged with assault and so, with her permission, Jeanne spoke to the police.

The police were on their way and so, for the time being, we were advised to give the man a wide berth. I didn't need telling twice. If he had assaulted his wife like this it wouldn't worry him in the least to lash out at any of the nurses. I quickly went around to the other staff to warn them what was happening (and asked Barry if he wouldn't mind hanging around until the police arrived). Everyone kept close watch on his every move, just in case things started to get out of hand, but thankfully the police arrived only a short time later. One female officer was sent through to question the lady and advise her that she would be taken to a place of safety, while another two were set to tackle the husband. They had been dealing with this particular family for quite some time now and it was common knowledge that the husband was a vicious bully and a well-known troublemaker.

I cannot begin to envisage what this oppressed woman had had to put up with over the years. I had never set eyes on the man before but I would certainly remember him in future. The police arrested him as soon as she told them what had happened and successfully removed him from the treatment area without any resistance or further incidents; he was obviously only the 'hard man' when it came to hitting his wife. He went out quietly with the police looking like butter wouldn't melt, but from the look on his face he clearly realised he was not going to get away with it this time.

His wife, on the other hand, was offered support and a place in a hostel for battered women until the police had decided definitely whether her husband was going to be charged and kept in custody. In the meantime, she was admitted to hospital overnight to ensure that she wasn't concussed after such a vicious beating. Their children were now grown up, so at least vulnerable youngsters weren't involved. Although, having said that, it was more than likely that this abuse had been going on for many years and the children would have either observed numerous such incidents, or could even have been on the receiving end themselves.

Domestic violence is much more common than many people realise, with children and adults being systematically mentally and/or physically abused for many years until the victims can tolerate it no longer. It is thought that at least one in four people experience domestic violence at some time in their life, yet less than half of them report the abuse to the police. The majority of abusers are men (although I have attended to one or two male victims during my career) who want to dominate and control their partner. Rape and sexual assault are common in such a partnership, with the wife too afraid to refuse intercourse and generally spending her life walking on eggshells in case she causes offence. Abuse is often kept hidden away behind closed doors; the victims being too frightened to complain or leave and their attacker presenting a completely different face to the outside world. The abusers commonly come across as friendly, sociable, outgoing personalities who are very easy to get on with; disguising a vicious inner self that none of their family and friends would believe possible. Not every victim is abused physically; emotional abuse is just as bad and can leave lasting mental scars.

A retired police officer, who had dealt with many cases of domestic violence, once told me that he had been called to a particular house on his patch dozens of times over a period of several years. But one day when neighbours had dialled 999 yet again, he and a colleague arrived in time to hear screaming, shouting and the sound of slamming doors coming from inside the house. Prior to this incident it was usual for them to find the wife battered and bleeding, although when questioned she was always adamant that she had been careless and tripped over the carpet or walked into a door. The fear on her face told a different story every time, but for the sake of her three young children she misguidedly felt that she needed to stay with their father, at least until they had all grown up and she knew that they were safe. The officer, a good, old-fashioned copper, had tried on a number of separate occasions to speak to her on her own, to see if he could find out what was really going on, and yet, each time he managed to get her alone, she wouldn't have a bad word said against her husband and stuck by him even to the point of blaming herself for being a poor wife. It seemed unbelievable that she was prepared to put up with this continuous abuse, but her children were her sole consideration and, as long as they were OK, she was prepared to wait until they were grown up and out of harm's way. Apparently, this attitude is a common one, and is based on self protection and fear. Understandably, the police sometimes find it very frustrating.

In this lady's case, however, after years of putting up with beatings that were becoming increasingly violent, the police had arrived in time to catch him in the act. He was observed through the window punching and kicking his wife around the lounge, so intent on assaulting her that he hadn't even noticed the officers arrive. Even more distressing was that their three children were on the landing upstairs, screaming and crying hysterically while they were forced to watch their mum being half killed. The two officers managed to gain entry into the house and restrain the husband before arresting him. The man was at long last banged up in a cell where he belonged, while the maternal grandparents looked after the children until their daughter was released from hospital. She decided there and then that she wasn't prepared to put up with such treatment any longer; enough was enough, and she brought charges of assault against her husband, who was convicted of grievous bodily harm and committed to prison. She also started immediate divorce proceedings.

The veteran police officer who had rescued this family heard nothing again from them for over twenty years, during which time he himself was seriously injured in a road traffic accident, sustaining serious spinal injuries that ended his career. He was having physiotherapy for his condition on a regular basis and, when he arrived for his treatment one day, a young female physiotherapist beamed and said hello when she saw him. She showed him into a cubicle and started to work on his legs and back, and then, after a few minutes of inconsequential everyday conversation, she suddenly said, 'You don't remember me do you?'

Taking a closer look at the young lady, he shook his head and had to admit that he hadn't a clue who she was. It turned out that she was the eldest of those three children watching from the upstairs landing as their mum was being pulverised by their thug of a father. With tears in her eyes she expressed her undying gratitude to this officer and said how much their lives had been transformed for the better since their father had been sent to prison. When he was eventually released, her parents had divorced and none of them had ever set eyes on him again.

Dealing with the result of domestic violence was a regular occurrence in Casualty and the staff themselves increasingly had to consider their own personal safety. When I started nursing it was far from unknown for a drunk to lash out, but levels of violence in the community around Wythenshawe and the general lack of respect for staff meant we had to remain particularly aware of the risks. Jeanne herself had memorably been in great danger during the previous summer when a man was brought in by ambulance after being found confused and apparently hallucinating. She took him into the first examination room and, for some instinctive reason, decided to leave the door slightly ajar. As she started to question the man in an effort to ascertain his problem, he suddenly produced a large kitchen knife from inside his jacket and threatened to kill her, saying he hated gypsies and that she looked like one.

Big Billy, one of the ambulance men, was passing the room and could immediately see that Jeanne was frightened, but couldn't see the weapon because the patient had his back to the open door. Stepping quietly into the room he could now make out Jeanne frantically mouthing the words, 'He's got a knife.'

Billy grabbed the man's hand and the knife fell to the floor as he was subdued. After being examined by the casualty officer, the man was referred urgently to the psychiatric department and subsequently sectioned under the Mental Health Act. He was assessed as being psychotic and judged to be extremely dangerous.

Thankfully, although Jeanne was shocked, she was uninjured and, after a large very sweet cup of tea, returned to duty. Counselling wasn't freely available to staff at the time so she just got on with the job. However, Jeanne was always partial to sweets and in the department if a grateful patient brought in a box of chocolates or a bag of sweets they would be left in a bowl under the reception counter for the staff to help themselves. Clearly still in need of a sugar boost to counteract the shock, Jeanne picked up a couple of what she thought were red Smarties and stuffed them into her mouth. Regrettably for her, they were in fact Brufen tablets (anti-inflammatories) that had been handed in to the receptionist by ambulance staff after being discovered in the trouser pocket of an elderly vagrant who had been brought in earlier. (The receptionist should actually have documented the tablets, handed them into the treatment room staff and eventually returned them to the patient, whose property they remained. She had intended to do this, but had been prevented from doing so at the time by sheer pressure of work and the volume of queuing patients, and the tablets had temporarily been forgotten about.) Jeanne's face was a picture when she found out and hysterical laughter among the staff banished any remaining serious atmosphere in the department.

Chapter 16

1.50am

Wendy and Christine soon came back from their break and took over from Kath and Theresa on the stretchers, who then went off for a break themselves. I was just about to call the next patients into the treatment area when a very sorry-looking individual stumbled in. Because of the apparent seriousness of his injuries, Stan had been brought straight through from reception and was under police escort. Covered from head to toe in blood, swearing obscenities at the two uniformed officers accompanying him, his appearance must have been quite disturbing to some of the other patients. After a cursory glance at his wounds revealed only superficial lacerations to his head that weren't considered to be a priority, I gave him a thick wad of gauze to wipe away the blood from his face and applied gauze and a crêpe bandage around the whole of his head, before asking him to sit quietly in the cubicle and wait until the doctor was free to examine him. In his condition it was simply easier and less disruptive to the other patients to keep him in the treatment area together with the escorting officers.

At the time we were all running around like headless chickens dealing with everything from heart attacks to dog bites, overdoses to broken noses and although each patient no doubt thought they deserved to be seen immediately, it was a physical impossibility. Dr Cross, as the sole casualty officer on duty, was ultimately responsible for dealing with all the acute emergencies in addition to the minor injury cases and, as such, his task was both daunting and time consuming. He had to assess each patient rapidly and if that patient's condition was considered serious, it was his job to stabilise them first before handing them over to the appropriate speciality. It was never a complete surprise, therefore, whenever a backlog of people waiting to be examined began to build up and, if the doctor on duty happened to be particularly slow, the situation could quickly deteriorate. Fortunately, Dr Cross was quick and confident in his diagnosis and referrals, and didn't stand any messing about when it came to dealing with drunks or complaining time-wasters.

All the examination rooms were occupied and only minutes earlier an ambulance had brought in yet another emergency cardiac patient who was critically ill and in need of urgent attention so, although Stan looked a bit gruesome, he had no option but to wait like everyone else.

The policemen were both local officers who were quite used to having to accompany detainees to Casualty and they could see how busy we were, so they realised they might be in for a bit of a wait. They knew we would always do our very best to deal with their prisoner as soon as we possibly could; after all, New Year's Eve was not only busy for us, but the police were also pushed to their limits dealing with drunken revellers and road traffic accidents, many of whom were liable to end up in Casualty with us at some stage. Being so obviously under detention was no doubt embarrassing for Stan, but it would have been even more so if he had been out in the main waiting room. At this time, though, there was little we could do about it; other patients had already been prioritised and that was that. At least he wasn't handcuffed to one of the officers, which was quite often the case.

After about twenty minutes or so, Stan started to become restless and every time a nurse or doctor caught his eye he jumped to his feet and waved his arms around trying to attract their attention, pleading for someone to come and help him so that he could go home. His raised voice could be heard all over the department and he was really starting to get on everyone's nerves. Other waiting patients who were bored and equally inebriated followed suit, shouting and chanting in unison that they, too, were fed up with waiting; the treatment area soon started to sound like the terraces at a football match. Before anybody could stop him, one booze-fuelled idiot staggered across the treatment area and burst into the resus room, where Dr Cross and the senior house officer from the medical ward were desperately trying to stabilise a patient who was in heart failure. This drunken tool had seen two doctors and a number of nurses running in and out of the room, so decided to have a look at what was going on for himself.

After gawping down at the unfortunate patient lying on the stretcher gasping for breath and surrounded by several staff, the drunk slurred, 'What are all you lot doing in here wasting your time on that sad bastard? He's obviously not going to make it, anybody can see that. We need a doctor out here to see to us.'

There was a sharp intake of breath from everyone who heard this drunken rant and I can hardly begin to describe the reaction this moron provoked with everyone in that room. One of the police officers in the treatment area started to make his way over to resus to see if he could help, but before he could get near him a large, athletic, young, male doctor (who was part of the medical team) grabbed the little numbskull by the scruff of his neck and the seat of his pants and frogmarched him to the swing doors leading back out into the treatment area. The policeman who had gone to help stood aside respectfully while the doctor, using the lad's body as a battering ram, slammed the drunk through the doors, before dragging him outside and warning him in no uncertain terms to stay there until he could behave like a normal human being. We congratulated the doctor on his actions and offered to keep him on as a bouncer for the rest of the night shift. He was fuming that anyone could be so thoughtless but turned and gave us a deep bow of mock appreciation as he quickly went back into resus.

After this outburst you could have heard a pin drop and Stan just sat there looking totally bewildered by the whole chain of events he had unwittingly set in motion. Up until this point, two or three of the other patients, all in various states of undress, had been wandering aimlessly around the treatment area, moaning and complaining loudly to their fellow sufferers about having to wait. Their main concern, of course, was that they were missing out on valuable drinking time, but after this incident the noise levels dropped dramatically as even their befuddled brains began to appreciate a little of the seriousness of what was happening behind the scenes.

Having worked in numerous Casualty departments over the years, I knew the constant whine from disgruntled patients about having to wait was pretty much commonplace. Sometimes it could be infuriating, particularly when everyone was running around like crazy and working as fast as they could, but overall it was something the permanent staff got used to and you became almost immune to the hassle. I suppose it is rather like living under the flight path of a busy airport; after a while, you simply don't hear the noise. On occasion I have been severely tempted to confront the people who are complaining loudest by dragging them into resus to see the result of a particularly hideous road traffic accident or the dead body of a young cardiac arrest victim and then watch their reaction.

Before too long, the two police officers once again found themselves having to remind Stan and several others waiting in cubicles to sit down and be quiet. No one was really taking too much notice of the officers so, as soon as I was free, I went over to Stan and had a careful look at his wounds. It took me the best part of ten minutes to clean him up sufficiently to get a much clearer idea of what was required, and was actually quite shocked when I saw the full extent of his injuries. Although they were only superficial, they stretched from ear to ear. Stan hadn't been knocked unconscious but I thought it prudent to check and document his head injury observations, just to make sure he was not concussed (or worse), and thankfully they were normal. Even though he was slurring his words, this appeared to be due to nothing more than the large amounts of booze he had been imbibing since early that afternoon.

Smelling drink on a patient's breath can be very mis-leading, though, and it is all too easy to dismiss the patient as being intoxicated. In my experience, anyone who comes into Casualty reeking of alcohol and complaining of a severe headache (whether they have had a head injury or not) should always have their observations checked in case the slurred speech/headache/dizziness are down to internal haemorrhaging or a clot rather than a result of the alcohol. It's not hard to make a mistake, especially when the casualty doctor is busy and pushed to the limit. They don't have a great deal of time to spend with each individual patient but, to cover all eventualities, it is always worthwhile for a nurse to record the patient's head injury observations for the doctor to at least consider.

After washing all the blood from Stan's head, he began to look a little less like Dracula and more like a human being again. Even though he was only about thirty years old, I have to say he looked much older. With short, dark, greasy hair that stank of stale beer and cigarettes, his face was unshaven and covered in acne or some other type of skin rash. Despite the freezing conditions, he was wearing only a T-shirt and jeans, and his teeth chattered with cold and shock as he began to shiver uncontrollably. Every item of clothing that he had on was heavily bloodstained and his T-shirt was torn in several places, clearly the result of being involved in a violent altercation, and even his shoes were badly scuffed with splashes of dried blood on them.

Having been examined by the doctor, the police officers escorted him into the suture room where I had been delegated to stitch him up. Once he was on the trolley, I covered him with a blanket and told him that the doctor would be in shortly. I stood there a minute or two, waiting for Dr Cross to come and administer some local anaesthetic into the numerous lacerations on Stan's head, but he had other ideas and was now busy in the next cubicle examining another patient. Calling him back, thinking he had forgotten about the injections, he grinned and whispered that the chap had got so much alcoholic anaesthetic already coursing around his body that there was little chance he was going to require any more tonight. He assured me the patient wouldn't feel a thing, but I wasn't too sure. Drunk or not, I didn't want to hurt Stan and neither did I want punching on the nose. I would just have to proceed carefully and play it by ear.

All the time I was setting out the instruments and organising the dressings, he was ranting and aiming abuse at the police in general, placing the blame entirely on them for having assaulted him. He was getting increasingly belligerent and the officers' presence seemed to be making matters worse, so I suggested that they wait outside in the corridor (where they could still guard both doors and hear him if he started to get difficult); perhaps that way he would calm down long enough to allow me to stitch him up without having to chase his head around the stretcher.

Watching them leave, Stan finally began to relax a little and started to tell me his tale of woe. He readily admitted that he had been out drinking for most of the afternoon and evening, but said that he had eventually decided to go home when he ran out of cash. Somewhat surprisingly, in view of his considerably inebriated condition, he had found his way home without any problem but then he couldn't find his front door key. After searching through his pockets several times without success, he eventually decided to wander around to the rear of the property, where he saw that the bathroom window had been left slightly open. In his drunken wisdom, he decided to climb up the drainpipe and crawl in through the window, or at least that had been his intention. Before he had got too far up, the next door neighbour, alerted by some strange noises outside, looked out and saw a shadowy figure halfway up the drainpipe and presumed someone was trying to break in. Because it was dark, the lady hadn't recognised her neighbour (who was by now stuck and hanging on for dear life) and, being a good citizen, she had dialled 999. As luck would have it, two police officers who happened to be in the next street had just finished dealing with an unrelated incident and were about to drive away when the call came through. Quickly driving around the corner, they pulled up and ran around to the back of the house, truncheons in hand, to catch this would-be burglar in the act. Unfortunately for Stan, the two were CID officers in plain clothes, so in his drunken state all he could make out were two young men, who he took to be muggers, rushing into his back yard dressed in dark clothes and carrying sticks. Although the pair identified themselves as policemen and showed him their warrant cards, Stan told me that, from his precarious position several feet off the ground, he couldn't think straight or understand what on earth they were talking about; he was just convinced that they were going to beat him up so decided to get his retaliation in first. He admitted that, as soon as he had managed to climb down from the drainpipe, he had lashed out at them in what he insisted was self-defence. He confirmed that the officers had definitely told him they were policemen but he hadn't believed them because they weren't in uniform and looked so young. After a bit of a free-for-all, the two officers had managed to restrain him, before placing him under arrest for attempted burglary and assaulting a police officer. They were about to take him back to the police station before common sense prevailed and he was brought to Casualty first to have his wounds checked out.

Unfortunately for him, he was going to need quite a lot of stitches in his head, so I warned him to keep very still. I approached the first few stitches quite gingerly, half expecting him to start cursing in pain because he hadn't had an anaesthetic, but he was so busy chatting he didn't even notice. Dr Cross had been correct, the alcohol proved to be a very effective anaesthetic, especially when combined with the adrenaline still rushing round his system. As he rambled on, I managed to put upwards of thirty stitches in his wounds over the next half hour without him even flinching.

Stan was adamant that he was going to put in an official complaint against the two officers who had injured him, and went on and on about the large amount of compensation he was now expecting to receive. I could well imagine the outcome of any claim; after all, he admitted to me (in front of the two officers who had brought him to Casualty) that he had attacked them first, even though his intention was to protect himself. I have to say that he was so drunk I had to take everything he said with a pinch of salt, but I documented everything just in case I was asked to make a statement at some point in the future. Once I had finished and the doctor was happy with his overall condition, the police took Stan back to the station to sober up. As I started to clean up the room to leave it ready for the next patient, Jeanne escorted in another equally inebriated punch bag and we both cast our eyes to the heavens. She left him with me to be cleaned up and went to find the doctor.

Dr Cross had been working at full speed, trying to keep on top of the numbers waiting for treatment. He went into the suture room to examine the new patient, a young man whose arm had been slashed with a knife, causing what appeared to be a three-inch superficial cut to his right forearm. After examining the wound, Dr Cross handed me the casualty card, which requested suturing by a nurse.

As a qualified nurse it was always emphasised that we were personally accountable for our own actions, so whenever I was asked to stitch a wound (regardless of the fact that the doctor had already examined the patient), I always checked it thoroughly myself. Hospital protocol dictated that nurses were only permitted to suture superficial lacerations, meaning the epidermis or first/outer layer of skin, and anything deeper required the doctor to carry out the task themselves.

Local anaesthetic had already been instilled into the wound by Dr Cross, so I was able to clean and inspect the cut without causing my patient any further discomfort. As the edges of the laceration opened up I noticed a long cut down the lad's tendon, which meant that the injury was actually far more serious and would probably require an operation. I apologised to the patient and, without going into detail, said that the doctor would just need to have another quick look at him.

When I shoved my head round the door looking for Dr Cross, there were several other doctors sat in the office writing up their records, having come down to Casualty from their various wards to see patients who had been referred to them by him. Not wishing to embarrass him in front of his colleagues, I asked if I could have a word in private. He must have been feeling the pressure because, completely out of character, he groaned at being disturbed and nearly bit my head off, 'For goodness sake, Joan, what do you want?'

I closed the office door so that patients couldn't hear and insisted that I needed to speak to him alone, but he wouldn't budge off his backside and told me to spit it out. I was feeling pretty tired myself at this stage so I thought: why should I worry?

'OK, fine, if that's what you want,' I said. 'The patient

you have just asked me to suture has a two-inch laceration down the length of his tendon, which I think you will find needs referral to the orthopaedic surgeons.' I then turned on my heel and walked out in a huff.

Looking a little flustered, Dr Cross followed me out. After re-examining the patient and seeing the laceration on the tendon for himself, the young patient was indeed referred to orthopaedics and admitted to the ward for surgery. Dr Cross very generously came over to apologise, which of course I accepted, but he didn't half get some good-natured stick from his colleagues, which was exactly what I had been trying to avoid.

Jeanne and I were the last to have our breaks and, as we sat nursing a slice of soggy quiche, she started to reminisce about the previous New Year's Eve, when her husband Jim had unexpectedly called in to the department to see her.

'Jim had been in the Naval Club all night and by midnight he was a bit tipsy and decided to come to Casualty to wish me and all the girls a Happy New Year. When he got here it was really busy; he couldn't see me anywhere and didn't just want to walk through into the treatment area, so he sat out in the waiting room until he recognised one of the staff.

'The waiting room was full of drunks who started whingeing about having to wait, and then one yob said, "That f**king fat slag of a sister won't let me be seen yet. When I see her I'll t**t her one!"

'Well, Jim stood up and punched him, saying, "Don't talk about my wife like that!"

'Next thing, all hell broke loose and someone rang the police. I heard the commotion and went to investigate, only to find Jim in the middle of the ruckus. I managed to drag him away and stick him in the linen cupboard until I found someone to cover for me, then took him home before the cops arrived. I nearly killed him. Oh, and I remember a really posh agency nurse, who was on that night, saying something about a "common" little man who had started all the trouble. I felt like punching her lights out myself!'

Knowing them both, I could just imagine the scenario, and can picture Jeanne dragging Jim home by the scruff of his neck in disgrace!

My feet were really starting to throb now, but our fifteen minutes were already up. I desperately wanted to get home to my bed, but there was no chance; it was still hectic with drunks backed up to the door so I resigned myself to another extended shift, as it was now highly unlikely I would be able to get off at 2.30am. My arms were stiffening up from carrying out the cardiac massage earlier in the evening, too, but I stopped feeling sorry for myself when my mind flashed back to the previous year and to an incident when a young girl's arms must have been feeling ten times worse than mine. It was late summer and I had only been on duty about thirty minutes when I took a telephone call from ambulance control to inform us there had been a serious accident involving a young boy, who was now impaled on some railings and an anaesthetist was urgently required to attend the scene. A small ad-hoc team from neighbouring Withington Hospital had volunteered to assist but their anaesthetist was busy so they had asked if we could provide one. Wythenshawe's own on-call anaesthetist, who had just dealt with a case in our plaster theatre, agreed to go out to the accident and asked me if I would go along to assist him. Sister was happy to give permission and ambulance control confirmed that they would arrange for us to be picked up.

Only minutes later we heard an approaching siren and a Greater Manchester Police traffic car screamed up to the ambulance bay. I jumped into the front seat and left the anaesthetist to scramble into the back with his equipment. I had already been involved in one previous high-speed vehicle transit, when accompanying a seriously ill patient being transferred to another hospital, and thought I had some idea what to expect, but being in the back of an ambulance at 50mph is a little bit different to being in the front seat of a high-powered police car forcing its way through traffic at far greater speeds. I closed my eyes and prayed, while the anaesthetist hung on for dear life in the back seat and tried to fend off a large pile of traffic cones that were piled up next to him. Our ordeal didn't last too long and we pulled up abruptly at a park behind a fire engine, an ambulance and a gathering crowd.

A young boy about eight years old had been up a tree collecting conkers but had slipped while attempting to climb down and had fallen backwards on to some railings, where a vicious spike had pierced his skull just behind his left ear. As he dangled there helplessly, a girl aged about thirteen had the great presence of mind to run and support his weight, which probably saved the boy's life. His friends had run to his home nearby to tell his mum, who alerted the emergency services. Although the Withington team had not yet arrived (but had much further to travel), the firemen were busy concentrating on cutting through the railings. They were extremely reluctant to take over from the girl who was holding him up for fear of causing further injury. The boy was moaning and drifting in and out of consciousness, while the girl was visibly trembling and about to burst into tears with the twin strains of maintaining her position and supporting his body for such a long time. The poor kid looked like she was about to collapse so I gently inserted my arms alongside her own and very carefully took his weight myself. She flopped down on the grass looking shocked and massaged her arms vigorously. The firemen continued to cut through the railings, while the anaesthetist monitored the boy's condition. When he was freed (with the spike still embedded in his head), two firemen and the ambulance men carried him carefully up the embankment, with me supporting his head, and put him in the waiting ambulance, just as the Withington team arrived. Once inside and strapped in, the doctor and I accompanied him in the ambulance with a police escort to Manchester Royal Infirmary, where he was scanned, x-rayed and stabilised before going to theatre and eventually making more or less a full recovery. As far as I was concerned, the young girl had been the hero of the day; without her quick thinking and immediate intervention I very much doubt there would have been such a successful outcome. The boy owed her his life!

At the time there were a few rumblings from the crowd who had gathered about the perceived delay in the medical team's arrival on scene, which was picked up by the local press. This resulted in considerable discussion about response times and the availability of emergency medical teams on standby for such incidents, so Dr Tony Redmond, the new consultant in charge of Wythenshawe Casualty, determined that he would organise a dedicated team able to respond to any future situations. The South Manchester Accident Rescue Team (SMART) was formed in 1987 and comprised a pool of senior doctors experienced in pre-hospital care acting as unpaid volunteers who would be available to respond to local incidents, particularly trapped/crushed victims, and who would train alongside the other emergency services. After being successfully established and called into action at local level whenever the occasion arose, the team's expertise was then to be tested at international level when invited to assist at the Armenian earthquake disaster in 1988 and then, only forty-eight hours after their return, at the scene of the Lockerbie air crash. The next such major incident SMART attended was the Iranian earthquake in 1990, when the team deployed included three A&E specialists, a general surgeon, a plastic surgeon, an intensive care specialist and three trained nurses.

Jeanne and I decided to have one last mince pie before tidying away our cups and plates ready to re-enter the fray.

Chapter 17

2.15am

As we walked back into Casualty, my sympathies went out to the few sober individuals sitting patiently waiting for attention in the midst of the mayhem. They must have thought that they had accidentally landed on another planet. We were just in time to see one of Jeanne's favourite regulars being taken into the suture room so we went over to deal with him first. This forty-year-old chap, who some of the casualty staff had nicknamed Tiny Tim because of his uncanny resemblance to the outlandish American singer/performer briefly famous in that era, loved his booze. It didn't matter whether it was New Year's Eve, or any other day of the year for that matter, he was a man on a mission to try and single-handedly drink the local pubs dry. The problem was, he never seemed to realise he'd had enough until he fell over. Not that he was ever aggressive or troublesome in any way; in fact, quite the opposite, as he tended to become a little amorous with the ladies as he staggered along trying to find his way from one pub to the next. I don't think I ever once saw him come into Casualty for any other reason than being paralytic, often after having fallen over in the road and been found there by a passerby, sleeping soundly.

Watching this man's attempts to manipulate his six feet three inch frame into the small suture room without further mishap was quite entertaining. He towered over Jeanne, who was only about five feet four, but was more than happy to cooperate with his nurse-of-choice and would do absolutely anything she asked without argument, no matter how drunk he was. I decided to hang around for another minute or two, just to make sure that she was able to get him on to the stretcher successfully. It was a bit of a struggle at first as his wobbly legs didn't want to coordinate with each other and seemed to be operating independently. Jeanne and I giggled as we eventually managed to get him lying flat and then, for his own safety, we pulled up the cot sides so he wouldn't fall off.

Dr Cross arrived and examined him, checking for signs of concussion, but apart from a rather nasty deep cut on the back of his head (which was already a huge mass of scar tissue from previous encounters), he seemed to have escaped serious injury this time. Looking at his casualty card, he had been discovered lying on his side in a ditch in the foetal position, snoring loudly. He was bleeding heavily but the laceration was partly hidden by his long, tangled hair, which made it difficult to see whether the wound was clean. In order to give Jeanne the opportunity to stitch him up, we needed to trim the hair around the cut and apply firm pressure to stop the blood flow. Jeanne got to work with her scissors and applied a fairly tight bandage to his head, all the time chatting away amiably to him as if he was one of her nearest and dearest. That was the thing I appreciated most about almost all the staff on Casualty, they invariably treated everyone exactly the same and patients were never made to feel uncomfortable, no matter how embarrassing the problem. About ten minutes later, the bandage was removed and it appeared to have done the trick, so she could now get busy with the sutures. At this point Jeanne was happy for me to leave her to it, so I wished her luck and went to see who the ambulance men were bringing in next.

The commotion in the department was pretty awful at this point and I felt ashamed at their behaviour when the next patient was wheeled in. A lady of about forty-five had been brought in complaining of dreadful abdominal pain; she looked desperately ill and to me appeared to be dying. Her husband had informed the ambulance crew that his wife was in the terminal stages of cancer and tonight she had suddenly started having severe pain and couldn't pass urine. Their GP had been requested to come out but was already busy elsewhere and unable to visit for at least an hour, so he had advised the husband to bring her to Casualty if the discomfort became too bad. The lady's face was etched with pain and her whole body was skeletal and cold as I introduced myself and assured her that the doctor would come to see her as soon as possible. I went to find Dr Cross who went over to see her almost immediately, treating the lady with great dignity and respect, in spite of the surrounding drunken hubbub. After examining her abdomen, he asked me to insert a catheter into her bladder, which thankfully gave her immediate relief. She squeezed my hand in gratitude and shed a tear, now a little more comfortable but visibly wincing at the sheer volume of noise and foul language emanating from the other patients. I could only apologise, but the sooner she could be sent home the better. Dr Cross gave me permission to organise some transport, although this unfortunately meant she would have to wait around until an ambulance became available. Anita in the meantime made them both a warm drink and volunteered to stay with this unfortunate lady until she was eventually sent on her way.

By now it was well after 2.30am and I should have been going off duty. Jeanne noticed the time and came over to tell me to get off home, but how could I? The place sounded and smelled like a bar room and I wouldn't have been surprised if we weren't all being affected by the fumes. I promised to stay until it had at least become a bit quieter. Famous last words.

Everybody had been so busy that I had hardly seen the other nurses to speak to for the last couple of hours, and I hadn't seen Cynthia in cas obs for more than a minute or so since the night shift came on duty. As I was staying a little longer, Jeanne decided to send the girls on another series of staggered ten-minute breaks. As for Dr Cross, apart from snaffling a couple of cold sausage rolls and a sandwich some-one brought through to him in the office earlier, he hadn't had any break at all since coming on duty at 10pm, so Denis's chocolate bars had certainly come in handy. In fact, they had been a godsend that helped to keep him going. He accepted a drink of tea and a mince pie which he consumed whilst writing his notes up, and he seemed happy enough, so we left him to get on.

When Jeanne and I eventually sat down together for the second time that night, she had a big smile on her face as she told me what Tiny Tim had been up to after I left the room. She had continued to make small talk while working on his cuts, until slowly realising that he had stopped listening and was eyeing her up and down intently.

Gazing at her adoringly through glassy eyes, he slurred his best chat-up line, 'Do you know, luv, you look just like Elizabeth Taylor?'

Jeanne preened herself and smiled graciously, accepting the compliment.

'Yeah,' he continued, 'all tits and arse and over fifty.'

It may have been a conversation stopper but Jeanne

refused to be mortally offended and was happy to share her moment with the others as well when we rejoined the action.

I think one of the other nurses had attempted to microwave a small meat pie at some stage during the evening, but must have got the timing wrong and succeeded only in cremating the unfortunate delicacy, which now sat black and crispy on top of an overflowing waste bin, and the smell was really getting to me. Burns were the only type of injury I never got used to throughout my career; it wasn't the appearance of them that affected me, although that was bad enough, but the smell of singed hair and burnt flesh. It seems to linger for days and, no matter how many times you shower or change your clothes, it is still there. The distinctive odour inevitably drags me back to when I was working at Blackpool Victoria Hospital in the late 1970s and was confronted by the worst burns victim I have ever had to deal with. Ambulance control rang to advise us that a middle-aged gentleman was en route to casualty suffering from horrific burns. By the time the approaching siren was heard, I was waiting with the casualty officer and another staff nurse at the main entrance to the unit, while all the necessary drips and drugs etc. were set up in readiness.

When the back doors of the ambulance were thrown open, the smell hit us like a sledgehammer. Declan was in deep shock, his face blackened by soot, and he grimaced in pain as we extracted him from the vehicle and rushed him into resus. I had dealt with burns on any number of occasions but had never seen any so extensive, and the sheets of skin dangling from his arms shocked me to the core, despite these being probably the least serious of his injuries. His clothes were unrecognisable and had largely melted onto his skin and, as we attempted to undress him and remove what remained, his skin peeled away with them, leaving patches of bright red, glistening raw flesh.

From the waist down Declan had third degree burns, i.e. both layers of skin (the thin epidermis and the thicker dermis) were black and completely dead. Thankfully, in one sense at least, these injuries were usually painless because the nerve endings had all been destroyed. The doctor used a small hypodermic needle to check the depth of the burns, but the patient could feel nothing. From the waist up, except for his face, Declan had suffered first degree burns, which although superficial were by far the most painful because the nerve endings were raw but still present, and he groaned at the slightest touch. As I was helping the doctor to put up drips and insert a urinary catheter, the poor man, who must have been in terrible pain, grabbed my hand and the sensation of his raw flesh and wet dripping skin against my own arm was simply indescribable. I spoke to him gently, trying desperately to reassure him, but also trying to ascertain details of any family members etc. before the strong pain relief which had been administered began to kick in and he became sedated. Declan was only able to tell me that he lived alone and came from Ireland, and that I should, 'Get a priest.'

The doctors tried to stabilise his condition but it was virtually impossible because the burns were so extensive, and we were certain that his death was imminent, so a priest was summoned urgently. Shortly afterwards a very young, fresh-faced Catholic priest arrived. Despite being pre-warned about the extent of the injuries, when the priest stepped behind the curtain in the resus bay, he staggered back and looked to me in panic, the colour draining completely from his face. Sister gave him a drink of water and we found him a gown to protect his clothes and a mask to partially obscure the smell. Our patient was now fading fast and the young priest gave him the last rites. Sadly, Declan was too badly burned to be given communion or even to be touched, and he died only minutes later. The priest was shaking as he came out of the cubicle and looked like he was going to faint, so we swiftly took him off into the staff room where he had his head unceremoniously pushed between his knees and he was given a cup of tea. That was his first time and I am willing to bet he isn't able to forget the smell either.

Back on the unit, Jeanne made sure that Jenny had managed to get something to eat and, thoughtful as ever, she also took a plateful of food round to the porters' room just in case any of them had missed out. I went back to continue helping out on minor injuries where Chris was trying to keep her temper with a female patient who was angrily demanding an ambulance to take her home, despite it having already been explained to her several times that ambulances were for emergencies only at night and that she would either have to wait until morning, ring a friend or get a taxi. While the argument raged, I kept out of the way and went to call in the next patient.

My next drunken volunteer needed to have his name called out three times before he finally staggered unsteadily into the cubicle and almost collapsed into a chair. He had been asleep in the waiting room and was, of course, well oiled. Looking at his casualty card, all that it said was that he had a problem with his arm. He stank of alcohol but otherwise appeared quite happy and cooperative, so all was going well so far. I asked him to show me his arm and questioned him as to how he had injured it. He didn't answer straight away because he was much too busy taking off his multiple layers of clothing. It was like peeling an onion as layer after layer was discarded and tossed carelessly on to the floor. He stood up and, just as I was trying to give him a hand to disrobe, he started to sway alarmingly, before falling back down on to the chair with a thump. Thinking that I would be there all night if I left him to it, I asked him to let me help. After shedding the last garment we finally got down to the arm in question. Apart from the tattoo of a rather well-endowed naked lady called Brenda, I couldn't see anything out of the ordinary.

271

'Where does it hurt?' I asked.

He looked puzzled as to why anyone should even consider asking such a stupid question and then, momentarily regaining his powers of speech, he answered, 'I want you to remove this.' Pointing to the tattoo, he added, 'I've had the bloody thing for years and I want to get rid of it.'

For a second or two I was speechless. I couldn't believe he had sat in the waiting room for the last two or three hours on New Year's Eve and genuinely expected us to start doing skin grafts on his arm in the early hours of the morning. I honestly didn't know what to say to the man and felt it would be far better if I kept my mouth shut and waited for Dr Cross to work his way down the line so I could see his reaction. He took the card out of the box and read it, looked at me and then at the 'patient', wrote something on the card and then went on to the next cubicle without speaking to either of us.

I took a quick look at the card, on which he had scrawled just two letters: GP. I informed the patient that his arm couldn't be treated in Casualty and that he needed to see his GP after the holidays. Without making any comment, he stood up, dressed himself, saluted, and wandered out of the treatment room towards reception and was gone. I assumed that he had left the building and gone home, but no. Twenty minutes later, I answered an internal telephone call from a rather distraught sister on the intensive care unit (ICU) asking if we had a porter to spare because a drunk had just wandered into their unit demanding they remove his tattoo. She said that at that precise moment he had plonked himself down next to an unconscious patient linked to a ventilator and was having a one-sided conversation with the machine.

After promising to try and find someone to help, I went to the porters' room but it was empty; they must have all been out on other jobs and none were even answering their bleepers. I quickly told Jeanne what had happened and she asked me if I was happy to go and sort him out, seeing as I had already dealt with him once. He had seemed fairly harmless when I saw him earlier, so I ran down the corridor. When I got to ICU, I found him still chatting away to the unresponsive figure in the bed. The staff understandably looked quite perturbed, and rightly so. They were worried that he might disturb their machinery but had been reluctant to confront him for fear of what he might get up to. How he had managed to get there under his own steam was a mystery, as ICU was a good long walk from Casualty in his condition.

However, when I went over to him and held out my hand saying, 'Come with me,' he dutifully stood up, took my hand and shuffled along beside me like a naughty schoolboy. It took us several minutes to get back to Casualty but, this time, after giving him a note telling him to see his GP, I saw him off the premises and watched him stagger away down the middle of the road singing his head off.

The mindless, hopeless and helpless were really coming out of the woodwork tonight and my next patient definitely fell into at least one of those categories. A teenage girl, who was dressed more appropriately for a hot summer's day, was sitting in a cubicle waiting for attention. The doctor had already checked her ankle (which she had hurt after stumbling on the icy pavement in her four-inch killer heels, as you do) and had decided that her injury was no more than a simple sprain. He had asked for the joint to be strapped and, when I went to apply some support to her ankle, she was sitting quietly with her left foot elevated on a foot rest, chewing gum and inspecting her nail varnish.

Once again I went down on my hands and knees. Clutching a roll of Elastoplast strapping, I applied it carefully from her toes to just above the ankle. When I had finished she smiled sweetly and said, 'Thanks, but why have you strapped my left foot, it's the right one that I've hurt?'

I could have slapped her. She was sitting there with her left foot up in the air, still wearing a stiletto and pop sock on her right foot, so what was I supposed to think? Yes, of course, I should have checked the casualty card, but after being on duty for hours you still retain the faint hope that your patient isn't quite as stupid as they look. The expression on Chris's face as she peered round the curtain of the next cubicle said it all as I dragged the now wasted strapping off the girl's leg and seriously considered wrapping it round her neck instead. I was not amused.

Chapter 18

4.00am

New Year's Eve is not always a time of fun and celebration. For many it brings the dread of facing yet another year alone or in debt and others are reminded of happier times with loved ones who are no longer with them. Tonight we had already dealt with two overdoses, but now two further cases were brought in by ambulance at more or less the same time. Both were females who had allegedly taken a combination of tablets and medicines.

Kath and Wendy were in resus dealing with the much more serious of the two cases. She had already been examined and had bloods taken by Dr Cross, who had then referred her on to the medics, but the second patient had arrived only ten minutes or so after the first and was now being wheeled into the overdose room hidden under a cocoon of blankets (it was easy to forget how cold it was outside). Theresa and I followed them in, just as the ambulance crew were about to go out again. They had already given Jenny the patient's details and, as if by magic, she appeared with the casualty card and a paper bag containing the two empty medicine bottles this lady was reported to have taken. Nothing was said, but I could tell from Jenny's face that something wasn't entirely straightforward. Looking at the patient's name on the casualty card, I groaned inwardly and showed it to Theresa, who pulled a face. Our overdose was none other than Barbara Barnes, our resident harridan whose dubious presence we had already endured earlier in the evening.

We called out her name in unison, insisting she come out from under her pile of blankets, where she had curled herself up into a ball and was gripping on to the covers for dear life. As she slowly emerged from the depths, Dr Cross held the empty containers under her nose and sternly demanded to know if she had taken anything other than the contents of the two bottles. As he asked the question, he handed the bottles across to show me what she had ingested, but the barely concealed grin on his face made me suspect the substances involved were not particularly life threatening. After a quick glance I passed them to Theresa who shook her head in despair – there was a half-empty bottle of Calpol (the one we had given to her son a few hours ago) and an empty bottle of Haliborange tablets that had expired three years before.

When questioned why she had taken these substances,

Mrs Barnes shrugged her shoulders but eventually admitted that it happened after she and her husband had been drinking. They had got into an almighty row, during which she had thrown a bottle at his head and then stormed off upstairs in a drunken strop. Deciding to teach him a lesson she had gone into the bathroom, grabbed the first bottles of medicine she had come across and swallowed them without a clue what she was taking. We assumed that one of the children had called for the ambulance because Mrs Barnes was too drunk to do so herself and her husband wasn't sufficiently concerned to come with her to hospital.

Dr Cross looked as if he was about to burst with frustration and could scarcely believe what he was hearing. He asked where her husband was now and if he knew what she had done. She again shrugged her shoulders and urged him to go away (or words to that effect), then crawled back under the pile of blankets, refusing point blank to answer any more of his 'stupid' questions. He decided to give her the vomit-inducing emetic medicine and told her that he would have to have blood samples taken to make sure she hadn't taken any other drugs that she wasn't telling us about. She swallowed the medicine grudgingly, pulling a face at the vile taste as it went down. It took another fifteen minutes or so before she threw up and then, after receiving the results of the blood tests (which were clear), it was decided to let her go home.

There was no way she had intended to kill herself but, to

be on the safe side, Dr Cross wrote a referral letter to the hospital psychiatrist asking him to carry out an assessment at some point; knowing full well that she probably wouldn't bother attending, but that was up to her. Theresa went to ring a family member who Mrs Barnes said would be willing to provide transport to take her home and I wrapped her in the blankets and left her waiting in the treatment area before clearing the room for the next patient.

Back in reception Jenny was asked by Dr Cross to find his next patient's previous casualty card. Because the old cards were stored in one of the back offices, this meant leaving the reception desk unmanned for a short time. No sooner had she set off on her quest than the telephone rang in reception. The doctor needed the card as a matter of urgency so Jenny ignored it, confident that if the call was important they would ring back. When Jenny got back to the desk, Mrs Barnes's daughter, another of our regulars, who was hanging around waiting to take her mother home, innocently informed her, 'Yer phone's bin ringin'!' The girl then collected Barbara from the treatment area and left.

A few minutes later, the phone rang again. The staff nurse on Childrens' Ward (who spoke ever so) wanted to advise Jenny that a GP had arranged for a young child to be admitted urgently, direct to the ward via Casualty. She was quite irate, though, and demanded to know who had answered the phone first time. In turned out that, when the staff nurse had asked if the receptionist was there, a female voice had replied, 'How the f**k should I know where she is, I'm only a f**king patient', and slammed the phone down. It didn't take a genius to work out what had happened or who was involved!

I'd just finished clearing up the overdose room when Jeanne asked me if I would have a look at a youth in reception who said that he had been hit over the head with a bottle and was bleeding like it was going out of fashion. When I went to find him, it turned out that he had suddenly decided to take himself off to the toilets so, since I had no intention of going looking for him, I sneaked into resus to see what was happening in there. Wendy and Kath were still busy with the other overdose victim – this woman had also had a row with her husband and, like Mrs Barnes, had decided to teach him a lesson. Unfortunately for her, the tablets she had decided to take were her husband's barbiturates, which were far more dangerous and potentially lethal. To make matters even worse, she had apparently taken the full bottle. Her husband had sat and watched his wife empty the bottle of pills (which he didn't realise were his) on top of the coffee table and then swallow them one by one, before washing them all down with the help of several large glasses of wine. He was too drunk to care what she was doing and fell asleep. By the time he woke up and found her semi-conscious on the sofa, she was very ill and barely coherent. She was now crying pitifully in resus, begging the medic and the two nurses not to let her die. Wendy and Kath feared there was nothing anyone could do as according to her blood test results, she had already absorbed a lethal amount of the drug. Drifting in and out of consciousness, she whimpered and asked for her husband, but he was nowhere to be seen and, according to the ambulance crew, had refused to come with her to the hospital.

The medical SHO had already taken a further series of urgent bloods and put up an intravenous drip. Wendy and Kath had attempted to pass a gastric lavage tube into her stomach to wash her out, but were having difficulty because her swallowing reflex was already inhibited by the drugs she had taken and absorbed. The on-call anaesthetist was sent for, who by the very nature of his job was used to intubating barely conscious patients, and was able to pass a tube without too much problem. He stayed with the patient to monitor her breathing while Wendy and Kath did the wash out. Once the procedure was completed, the patient was transferred immediately to intensive care. To my knowledge, even though her husband had been informed of the seriousness of her condition, he never made the effort to be with her and we heard the next day that tragically she died only hours after admission.

When the patient I had been waiting for finally emerged from the toilet, I took him into a cubicle to clean up the wound in order to assess the injury. His mate, who had arrived with him, insisted on coming in, too. While I was cleaning him up, I asked how he had injured himself. Glancing first at his friend, he told me that someone had thrown a broken bottle at him which had caught him on the head. As I checked through his hair I could see dozens of beads of laminated glass (which, from long experience of car crash victims, I knew without doubt, were from a car windscreen). I went to fetch a comb, gave him a paper towel to hold in front of his forehead and asked him to lean forward. Slowly and carefully, making sure I didn't cut him further, I teased out the glass, which he caught and collected on the towel, and then, after I had completed my task, I presented the broken glass to him and asked if he would like to change his story.

Picking up one of the pieces I pointedly said, 'This is windscreen glass, not from a bottle, and although it doesn't matter to me how you got the cuts, the doctor will need to assess just how hard you have hit your head.'

He said nothing. Unknown to me, two traffic policemen had arrived in Casualty looking for a couple of young lads who had stolen a car. After following them for several miles they had lost them in the warren of streets on the Wythenshawe estate. After cruising around the area for about half an hour, they had come across the damaged vehicle abandoned in a back alley. On closer inspection they could see the car windscreen was smashed and one of the officers noticed fresh blood on the dashboard on the driver's side. Presuming that at least one of the occupants was injured, they had considered the possibility of them being in Casualty. The two police officers had overheard our conversation, so after the lad had been seen by the doctor and stitched up by me, both lads were arrested as they left the building.

I was feeling completely shattered by now but there were still lots of patients to be dealt with. Many of them were so fed up with waiting they had fallen asleep curled up on the floor of the waiting rooms. A drunk wearing a bright pink tutu, sparkly tiara and rugby boots was slumped in a chair, legs akimbo and head back, snoring for England, a droopy magic wand clutched firmly in one huge fist. At well over six feet in height, unshaven and weighing probably twenty stones, none of the other waiting patients could quite bring themselves to wake the man to tell him that one hairy testicle had escaped from his Calvin Klein boxers and was peeping mischievously at them from behind his short frilly skirt. An equally large and equally inebriated Superman was snuggled up next to him on a wheelchair, dribbling gently, his costume stretched so tightly across his ample beer belly that it looked like a beach ball wrapped in cling film. The things you see when you haven't got a camera!

As I dragged myself back to the stretcher side, Jeanne noticed the clock and came over to tell me to go home. It was now just after 5am and she warned me that if I didn't go now, then I would probably still be here when the day staff came on duty at 8am. To be honest, I had got beyond caring, but I promised to see to just one or two more patients and then I'd be off.

The first stretcher case I had to deal with was a middle-aged man who suffered from chronic asthma. He'd gone out to a small party at a friend's house but had forgotten to take his inhaler with him. The house was very warm and lots of people were smoking and, as the night progressed, his chest felt ever tighter, until he found it increasingly difficult to get his breath. He was forced to go outside for some fresh air, which temporarily eased his discomfort, but before too long, the other guests started coming up to him asking if he was OK. He initially shrugged them off, not wanting to cause a fuss, but was soon desperately gasping for air and wheezing loudly, before eventually sinking to his knees in distress. His host called for an ambulance and now he was in Casualty, sitting with his legs over the side of the stretcher struggling to breathe. Dr Cross listened to his chest, questioned him about his general medication and then prescribed a Ventolin nebuliser. Chris went to sort that out while I checked the patient's blood pressure and pulse rate.

After only a few minutes on the Ventolin, he began to breathe much easier. Chris and I left him to settle down, asking his wife to come and sit with him while he completed the treatment, and giving her a buzzer to call us if needed.

Ten minutes later, Chris and I returned to check on him and walked into the choking cloud of cigarette smoke that filled the room. Not only was the man's wife smoking as she sat next to the oxygen supply (with the inherent danger of fire or even explosion) but the patient was sitting with his mask in one hand and a glowing cigarette in the other! Dr Cross lost his temper when we told him and gave them both a stern lecture on the dangers not only to their own health but ours, too. They looked totally bemused and couldn't understand why we had a problem with their behaviour. The chap was still wheezing like mad but reluctantly extinguished his fag before completing his treatment. The wife was shown the door and instructed, in no uncertain terms, to stay outside until her cigarette was finished and never to smoke in hospital again. She looked at Dr Cross like he was off his trolley. Chris and I were astounded at the pair's foolishness, but kept our own counsel for fear of getting into trouble for telling them what we truly thought.

My final patient was a teenage girl who was brought in while having a panic attack, which started at a friend's house. She had never experienced anything like it before and was convinced she was about to die. An ambulance had brought her in and, before leaving, the crew had given her a paper bag to breathe into, but she was very agitated and couldn't understand what purpose the paper bag was supposed to achieve. When a panic attack occurs it is characterised by short, erratic breathing that creates an increase of oxygen into the bloodstream. A paper bag held firmly over the nose and mouth reduces this oxygen level and allows the symptoms to disappear fairly quickly. Panic attacks are not life threatening but, to anyone who has ever experienced one before, they can certainly feel like it; often coming on without warning, they promote a feeling of intense fear or discomfort. Although they usually last for only a brief time, during that time the recipient can feel like they are on the point of having a heart attack or a nervous breakdown. These attacks usually vary from person to person but can be triggered by such diverse experiences as phobias, significant life-changing experiences (divorce, bereavement and illness), caffeine intake and stress. The symptoms can vary from palpitations, sweating and shortness of breath, to irrational fear and a sense of impending death. Medication is only one of several methods to control these attacks but it doesn't actually resolve the problem; learning to relax the muscles and control breathing (yoga is really good) can prove particularly useful when practised regularly.

I chatted to the patient, trying to reassure her that she would soon settle down and feel much better. I did my best to explain panic attacks to her but, in all honesty, she wasn't really listening and insisted that she was not stressed or worried about anything, and now just wanted to go home. The girl's friend stayed with her but, without wanting to sound too critical, she was neither use nor ornament and was only interested in getting back to her friends at the party. Dr Cross came in to check the patient out and could see that she was beginning to settle. He also tried to explain to her what was happening, but the girl again insisted that she could think of no relevant factors that may have brought on the attack. He questioned her caffeine and alcohol intake and asked whether she smoked. The girl scoffed at the idea that any of these could be the cause, although when she told him just how much she actually drank he was horrified.

Once she started feeling better, the girl quickly discarded the paper bag, jumped off the stretcher and demanded transport home. I told her that only emergency ambulances were on duty at night but I would ring a friend or a taxi for her if she gave me a number. This wasn't good enough for her; she insisted on being taken home by ambulance. It simply wasn't going to happen and I told her that her only alternative would be to wait until 9.00am when the transport ambulances came on duty, but that she was likely to have a very long wait even then. She jumped to her feet, swearing and cursing, then called me an effing bitch and gave me a V-sign as she stormed out with her friend trailing along in her wake.

'And a Happy New Year to you, too,' I shouted after her, slamming the door in disgust.

That was it, I'd had enough! My feet were killing me and every joint ached. I sought out Jeanne and told her I was off. She thanked me for staying on and very kindly offered to terminate her own shift early and go home instead of me, should I have an overwhelming desire to stay on and continue saving lives, but I decided to decline her generous offer! Waving goodbye to all the other girls I went into the changing room to collect my belongings from my locker. Looking out of the window, a million stars were shining brightly in a crystal clear sky and the moon reflected on the glassy pavements, making me shiver involuntarily and wrap my coat even more tightly around me as I pushed my way through the scrum around the reception desk and ventured outside, delighted I could now trust their care to the tender mercies of my colleagues.

Getting into my car felt like getting into an industrial freezer unit and when I turned the ignition key the engine gave an insignificant grunt, then nothing! The battery was as dead as a doornail. I started to feel distinctly sorry for myself as I wandered dejectedly back into reception, wondering what best to do next. I didn't think Bill would be best pleased to get a phone call asking him to pick me up, my AA membership had run out and I hadn't yet got round to renewing it and, assuming I could even get a taxi, I didn't fancy leaving my car in the car park outside any longer than necessary if I ever wanted to see it again.

Then I saw my saviour. Ken, one of the local coppers who had been around earlier, had just called in as he was passing to check that we were OK. Seeing my damsel in distress expression, he listened to my tale of woe and gallantly came to my rescue. Taking my keys he said that he had some jump leads in his patrol car and ten minutes later my knight in shining armour came back to announce that my little yellow peril had sprung back to life. Expressing my undying love and devotion for his kindness, I hurried out and hit the road.

Heading back down Southmoor Road towards the dual carriageway, my Mini did a little shimmy to remind me of the dangerous road conditions and I negotiated the round-about on to Brooklands Road with great care. There wasn't another car on the road at that point, only a drunk staggering along on the pavement having a conversation with himself, who stepped out and attempted to flag me down. No chance. Gently swerving around him, I continued on my way down the long, straight road, appreciating the frozen beauty of the halo of light around each glowing street lamp surrounded by heavily frost-laden branches.

Pulling into the drive at home about ten minutes later, I was glad to finally switch off my engine and quietly open the front door. I was particularly thankful that the central heating was on, as I could now hardly feel my hands and my feet were like blocks of ice.

I decided to go straight up to bed but happened to glance in the hall mirror and was horrified to see a stain on the front of my new coat. For a split second I thought a slug or a snail had caused the long silvery trail which glistened against the smooth black wool, but instantly dismissed the possibility. Taking off my gloves, I brushed the mark and scratched at it with my fingernail, but it wouldn't shift. Licking my finger I rubbed it vigorously. I was starting to make an impression on it so I licked my finger again to repeat the exercise.

And then I remembered bumping into Jack Barnes, the apprentice thief, as he tried to escape.

The little boy with the snotty nose . . .

Oh well, the coat would just have to wait, my bed was calling and I could hear my personal hot-water bottle snoring gently upstairs.